EMPEROR PENGUIN AND CHICK, ANTARCTICA

ELEPHANT, BOTSWANA

National Geographic's
Last Wild Places

Prepared by
The Book Division
National Geographic Society
Washington, D.C.

BIG BEND NATIONAL PARK, TEXAS

National Geographic's
Last Wild Places

Authors

Elisabeth B. Booz
Patrick R. Booz
Suzanne Chisholm
Noel Grove
Michael Parfit
David Yeadon

Published by

The National
Geographic
Society

Reg Murphy, *President
and Chief Executive Officer*
Gilbert M. Grosvenor,
Chairman of the Board
Nina D. Hoffman,
Senior Vice President

Prepared by

The Book Division

William R. Gray,
Vice President and Director
Charles Kogod,
Assistant Director
Barbara A. Payne,
Editorial Director

Staff for this book

Charles Kogod,
*Project Editor
and Illustrations Editor*
Kevin Mulroy,
Text Editor
Cinda Rose, *Art Director*
Anne E. Withers,
Senior Researcher
Annie Griffiths Belt,
Contributing Picture Editor
Sophie Elbrick,
James B. Enzinna,
Susan A. Franques,
Kimberly A. Kostyal,
Robin Tunnicliff,
Researchers

Margery G. Dunn,
Consulting Editor
Elisabeth B. Booz,
Patrick R. Booz,
Noel Grove,
Kim Heacox,
Doug Lee,
David Yeadon,
Picture Legend Writers
Carl Mehler, *Map Editor*
Joseph F. Ochlak,
Map Researcher
Debbie Freer, GeoSystems
Global Corporation,
Map Production
Lewis R. Bassford,
Production Project Manager
Richard S. Wain,
Production
Meredith C. Wilcox,
Illustrations Assistant
Kevin G. Craig,
Editorial Assistant

Dale M. Herring,
Peggy J. Purdy,
Sam Taylor,
Staff Assistants

Anne Marie Houppert,
Indexer

Manufacturing
and Quality Management

George V. White,
Director
John T. Dunn,
Associate Director

Library of Congress CIP data:
page 272

COURTING ALBATROSS, SOUTH GEORGIA ISLAND

Contents

Foreword

I've long believed in the John Muir maxim, "The clearest way into the Universe is through a wilderness." His statement takes on more weight now because that wild door to the universe has been slowly closing since he called it to our attention at the turn of the century. Ours may be the last generation with the opportunity to insure that wild places will always beckon to humankind, offering us a way to better understand our role in the cosmos.

As a professional conservationist I have long worked to save natural areas, and with the help of generous and imaginative people more than 2,000 places have been set aside. My focus has been principally in the United States, but thanks in part to this book I now see opportunities for global preservation that can benefit people everywhere. I have been deeply moved by the scope and beauty of undeveloped areas remaining around the world as seen in these pages. The photographs illustrate the splendor of highly diverse landscapes, and the texts detail their uniqueness. I was struck by the vastness of Australia's Queensland, fascinated by the richness of Africa's Okavango, heartened that on our own crowded North American continent there are still areas as untrammeled and forbidding as Wrangells-St. Elias and Kluane.

Beyond their compelling beauty, these wild gems are important to us for very practical reasons. With fresh water constituting only 3 percent of the moisture on this planet—and most of that locked up in Arctic ice packs—the filtering and purifying capabilities of wilderness areas are becoming critical in our polluted world. As we continue to lose species whose potential benefit to us has not yet been documented, undeveloped areas become valuable banks of biodiversity. Many wild creatures that we enjoy observing migrate over considerable distances, and the retention of large areas of natural habitat allows them to continue a way of life that we have often blocked or altered.

Finally, we need these wild places for our spiritual renewal. We're a clever species, and sometimes we become overly impressed by the genius of our comforts and technology. Humanity could use a dose of humility once in a while, and to me it is humbling to see how the natural world works so well. Left alone it achieves a venerable balance, which cannot often be said of areas touched by the hand of man. For that reason, even though I will never see most of the places revealed in this book, it is a joy just knowing that they exist. As the author Wallace Stegner warned us years ago, "Something will have gone out of us as a people if we ever let the remaining wilderness be destroyed."

This book echoes a memorable issue of *National Geographic* magazine in 1916. Entitled "Land of the Best," it depicted the bountiful gifts that nature had bestowed on the United States. The issue played a role in the eventual creation of our National Park System, now replicated in more than 130 nations. It is my hope that *National Geographic's Last Wild Places* will similarly play a role in helping save the world's remaining Edens.

America takes pride in its wilderness, just as all nations do. We need to protect all of the world's remaining wild places and to cooperate with developing countries that need assistance with preserving fragile ecosystems. I can think of no greater impetus toward world peace than the vision of nations working together to save the natural heritage that benefits us all.

Patrick F. Noonan
Chairman, The Conservation Fund

GREAT BARRIER REEF MARINE PARK, QUEENSLAND, AUSTRALIA

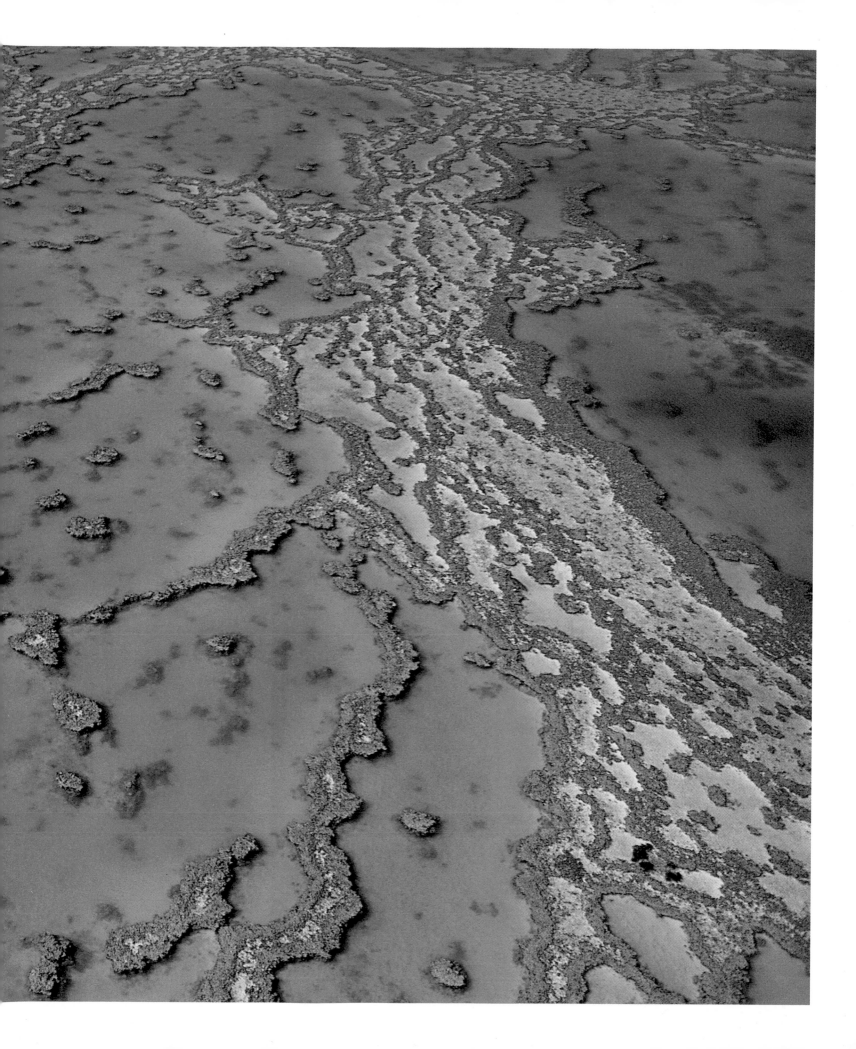

MOUNT MCKINLEY, DENALI NATIONAL PARK, ALASKA

RAIN FOREST, VICTORIA, AUSTRALIA

BLACK CAIMAN, MANU NATIONAL PARK, PERU

TREES SILHOUETTED AT SUNSET, SERENGETI, TANZANIA

Mediterranean Sea

TUNISIA

MOROCCO

WESTERN
SAHARA

ALGERIA

LIBYA

EGYPT

Red Sea

S A H A R A

Tassili-n-Ajjer
National
Park

MAURITANIA

MALI

Aïr and Ténéré
National
Nature Reserve

NIGER

ERITREA

S A H E L

SENEGAL

GAMBIA

Niger

BURKINA

CHAD

Lake
Chad

SUDAN

DJIBOUTI

GUINEA

GUINEA-
BISSAU

SIERRA
LEONE

LIBERIA

CÔTE
D'IVOIRE

GHANA

BENIN

TOGO

NIGERIA

Gashaka-Gumti
Reserve

ETHIOPIA

Bale
Mountains
N.P.

EQUATORIAL
GUINEA

SAO TOME
AND PRINCIPE

CAMEROON

CENTRAL AFRICAN
REPUBLIC

Dzanga-Sangha
Dense Forest Reserve

Dzanga-
Ndoki N.P.

Nouabalé -Ndoki
National Park

Ruwenzori N.P.

Masai Mara
Reserve

SOMALIA

Virunga
N.P.

UGANDA

KENYA

GABON

CONGO

ZAIRE

Volcanoes N.P.

Serengeti
National
Park

RWANDA

BURUNDI

Congo

Lake
Victoria

Ngorongoro
Conservation
Area

INDIAN

OCEAN

Mount
Kilimanjaro
19,340 ft
5,895 m

SEYCHELLES

ATLANTIC

OCEAN

Lake
Tanganyika

TANZANIA

COMOROS

ANGOLA

MALAWI

Lake
Malawi

ZAMBIA

Chobe
N.P.

MOZAMBIQUE

MADAGASCAR

Zambezi

Skeleton
Coast
Park

Namib Desert

Okavango
Delta

Boteti
River

Makgadikgadi
Pans

ZIMBABWE

NAMIBIA

BOTSWANA

KALAHARI
DESERT

0   600 Mi
0   1000 Km

SOUTH

AFRICA

SWAZILAND

LESOTHO

Africa

by Noel Grove

"Going up that river was like traveling back to the earliest beginnings of the world," wrote Joseph Conrad of the Congo in *Heart of Darkness*. Even today, something in the broad sweep of savanna, in the dank thick knots of vegetation, in the large herds wandering unfenced and the raw dramas of survival and death that follow them, recalls an earlier time. Africa looms huge in our minds as a place yet untamed, a land where nature, not man, often holds sway.

While we hearken to the past, Africa faces the thundering present, a population at least six times larger than it was at the turn of the century and growing at 3 percent a year. Towns bulge into cities, savannas sprout farms, and free-ranging wild herds are culled for damaging croplands.

But wild areas remain. Africa still has vast tracts so rugged or with so little agricultural promise that the tide of civilization has yet to wash them away. The mix of unspoiled ecosystems is astoundingly diverse. The Sahara spreads over a third of the continent and contains hardy forms of life. Just below it lies the thorny acacia savanna of the Sahel, giving way eventually to rich grasslands with their wealth of animals. Extravagant wetlands line the Mediterranean, steamy mangrove swamps fringe the Red Sea and Indian Ocean, and the freshwater marshes of Sudan and Botswana are unparalleled. The tropical forests are the Africa of our Tarzan imagination, jungles that line permanent streams and are so dense in parts of central Africa that they remain unexplored.

All are indexes to a world that once existed on this planet, treasuries of wild grace and scenic wonder. In Africa and elsewhere, efforts are under way to save these remnants, lest all our yesterdays end up looking too much like today.

Okavango

Most rivers run to the sea, but the Okavango runs to a desert and disappears in the hot sands. In that journey between rainfall and evaporation it waters an Eden that has been called "the last of Old Africa," a wild oasis in the middle of the Kalahari Desert that draws animals of many species into a tight menagerie. The Okavango Delta of Botswana is the largest inland wetland in the world, and the largest remaining wilderness in southern Africa.

This garden of greenery results from a fortuitous coincidence of local rainfall and water flow from far away. The land around the delta has its own rainy season, from October to March, which greens up the Kalahari so grazing animals can wander in its vastness. But the water holes and grazing soon dry up in the desert, leaving animals desperate for food and water. The water finally arrives after a journey of a thousand miles.

During February and March substantial rains have been soaking the highlands of Angola, far to the northwest. Waters from that deluge take nearly half a year to cross the border into northern Botswana as the Okavango River. When the flood from the north arrives, it flows into marshes, pumping in nutrients and reoxygenating the waters, eventually spreading out in a fan 150 miles wide, covering broad grasslands with a thin sheet of water, renewing vegetation, and drawing the hungry and thirsty from the surrounding desert like a magnet. Any water left finally succumbs to desert heat, but by that time an area larger than Connecticut has been renewed and irrigated.

The gift from the north takes some five months to flow from the top of the delta to the lower grasslands, which means the area has not one but two wet seasons. The first comes from the region's own rainfall; the second from the charge of northern water that arrives just as the surrounding countryside is beginning to dry up. The animals benefiting from this double dose of moisture are as numerous and diverse as they once were throughout much of the continent.

Hippos by the hundred lounge in deep pools and bulldoze paths through the reed beds, emerging on land at night to graze. Crocodiles feed on fish, snakes, turtles, waterbirds, and any careless mammals they can snatch from the banks. Sharing the waters in a precarious existence are some 80 species of fish, preyed on not only by the toothy reptiles but also by

Creatures great and small share a water hole in Chobe National Park in northern Botswana. When rains stop in surrounding plains, elephant and antelope join a menagerie of species, here and in the nearby Okavango Delta region, an oasis offering the gift of life during the dry season.

fishing eagles, anhingas, and other waterfowl drawn to an aquatic feast.

For sheer tonnage, the largest group of delta dependents are the nomadic herbivores that return to this ark of moisture when the plains turn dry. The largest collection of elephants remaining in Africa, some 65,000, come to eat and drink and wash off the dust of the Kalahari. Zebra and Cape buffalo drift here in herds of rumbling thunder. The mix of grazing types is unmatched anywhere. Desert antelope such as gemsbok and springbok mix with wetland species such as lechwe and waterbuck. Wildebeest and impala, plains animals, mingle with kudu and sable, beasts of the woodlands. One aquatic antelope treads where others cannot follow; the hooves of the sitatunga are long and splayed, allowing it to venture onto the dense mat of papyrus that is suspended in the water. Feeding off the concentration of game are legions of predators: lions, leopards, cheetahs, hyenas, and wild dogs.

Man is also a predator here and a user of the delta as well. Tribal villages lie scattered along the banks and on some of the larger islands, and residents hunt and fish, gather edible plants, and farm. For thousands of years they have been little more disruptive than other delta dwellers.

Not even the introduction of trophy hunters from abroad, carefully restrained by government quotas, makes a large dent in the animal populations. More dangerous to life in the delta has been the successful spraying of the tsetse fly, carrier of sleeping sickness that can be deadly to people and cattle but not to wildlife. Until recently, the fly has kept the delta a wild domain.

With the tsetse all but eradicated, a government eager for foreign exchange considers enlarging its beef industry to increase exports to Western Europe. No longer threatened by the tsetse, herders look covetously toward Botswana's only permanent surface water. Overgrazing by cattle and goats, especially in times of drought, can remove vegetation needed by wildlife. Fences to separate wild herds from domestic block migratory routes used for millennia. Diamond miners using processes that require large amounts of water also eye the delta. There is talk of channelizing some of the water for agricultural use in Botswana, and talk by nations upstream of damming the river for agricultural and industrial use. Any of these uses could mean trouble for a land now well watered. Together, they could doom thousands of thirsty wild mammals.

The delta may yet retain its vitality. Seventeen percent of Botswana's land is set aside as national parks or game reserves, one of the highest percentages of protected land in the world. Government officials sensitive to wildlife needs are also aware of the income brought in by tourism and trophy hunting. A growing number of environmentalists in the nation, including the Botswana people, may help the Okavanga Delta remain a gem in the crown of wild Africa.

A rambling river that seems to lose its way, the Okavango in flood creates many lagoons and channels on the tabletop terrain (opposite, above). Silt collecting on raised termite mounds builds islands of vegetation. The thin liquid sheet over the land nurtures verdant plant growth, including the night-blooming water lily, which closes in daytime (opposite, below). An antelope supremely adapted for the delta's rank swamps, the sitatunga's long, splayed hooves allow it to bound over the tops of soggy papyrus beds to escape danger.

Spreading the Gift of Life

Fault lines formed by the shifting of geologic plates two million years ago created the basin that holds the Okavango Delta. As it spills its banks in northern Botswana, the river is contained within two parallel fault lines, forming the panhandle of the delta. After 60 miles water spills over the Gomare Fault that runs crossways to the flow, and thereafter spreads more than 5,000 square miles. If any water is left after transpiration and evaporation, it runs up against another fault, the Thamalakane, at the bottom end of the delta. Forced again into one channel, the water flows southeast in the Boteti River until it disappears in the dry, salty Makgadikgadi Pans.

Water lilies decorate shallow backwaters throughout the delta, their stems uncoiling at flood stage to lift blossoms above the surface. Within days the stems retract and the submerged flowers release seeds. In the northern woodlands, trails lead to a clay pan (opposite), a reliable water hole in the wet season only.

Evening whets the appetites of four lionesses, alert for game in tall grass of the Okavango. Likely prey, svelte impalas bound past a termite mound in daytime (opposite).

In a strategy aimed at avoiding the claws of the big cats, impalas move into deeper cover at night, when the sound of lions approaching can be heard more easily.

Ndoki

The words "darkest Africa" never rang more true than in the central African region known as Ndoki. In its humid, tropical, lowland rain forests the sun seldom reaches the forest floor, leaving all but rare clearings in a state of perpetual gloom. Heat, dense vegetation, deep water, and insects all conspire against human presence so that even the forest-wise Pygmies stay mostly on the fringes of an area about the size of Belgium.

Being kept in the dark has its advantages. Ndoki may be one of the few places unchanged since man began putting his mark on earth. Animals encountered by the handful of expeditions that have entered Ndoki in this decade give indications that they have never before seen a person. As a result, the jungle may be teeming with more wildlife per square mile than in any other place on a continent known for large collections of wild animals.

Tropical lowland forests cover 6 percent of earth's surface and have long been known to hold the richest assemblages of life-forms anywhere. After South America, Africa has more intact tropical forests than any other continent. The largest clump of it lies in the Congo Basin, an area that touches the nations of Zaire, Congo, Central African Republic, and Cameroon, but none is less explored than the 7.5 million acres of the Ndoki River watershed. The region is almost inaccessible. Swamps thick with underbrush border it on the south and east, steep hills lie to the north, and along the west side runs the Ndoki River, too littered with vegetation to navigate easily, too deep to wade. Insect bites can cause fever and nausea. One form of malaria can kill a person within hours of the first attack.

Behind those barriers lies a world of wonders, for those who can survive it. Towering malapa trees shield open areas beneath them, carpeted with their long, oval leaves. Mahogany trees measure 50 feet around with high, fluted buttresses at their bases, so draped with ferns and vines that their soaring tops cannot be seen. Parrots, bats, great blue turacos, shrikes, and countless other birds course through the foliage. Some of the insects are spectacular: huge moths, six-inch mantises, nine-inch walkingsticks.

And mammals. Ndoki holds some of the most important wildlife populations left in West Africa, several of them endangered. It is home to large herds of forest elephants, smaller than those of the savanna and with roundish ears. Little is known of them, but the largest free-ranging herd may

Steeped in mystery, Nouabalé-Ndoki National Park simmers in the tropical heat of the Congo. Virtually unexplored, jungles here and in neighboring Central African Republic offer sanctuary to countless species, some endangered. Buffer zones and limited access protect them from loggers and tourism.

be in this forest complex. Moving in paths cleared by the pachyderms are dwarf forest buffalo. Lowland gorillas and chimpanzees, in serious decline, wander here in abundance with no fear of man. Encountering the first humans to survey the unknown area, gorillas charged in warning but did not flee. Chimpanzees, hunted elsewhere, stared at the intruders from close range, as we might marvel at aliens from another planet. Nine species of monkeys share the forest with the larger gorillas and chimps, and the density in some areas is 50 monkeys per square mile. Blue duikers—small forest antelope—probably number a hundred per square mile, and share the forest

Ndoki

with bush pigs, sitatungas, the shy, striped bongo antelope, numerous smaller animals, and predators such as golden cats and leopards.

Although they remain unaware of an outside world, their long seclusion may be ending. Logging concessions almost completely surround Ndoki. West Africa may already have lost three-quarters of its woodlands to logging activities, as developing countries see plentiful timber as their most valuable resource. As logging creeps closer, the roads built to accommodate removal of the wood make remote locations easier to access. Poachers, especially those seeking elephant ivory, have already made kills on one side of the Ndoki River, and eventual invasion into the dense sanctuary would be only a matter of time.

To conserve the wildness of Ndoki, Congo has declared nearly a

million acres as Nouabelé-Ndoki National Park. It connects with two other slightly smaller protected areas in the Central African Republic, Dzanga-Ndoki National Park, and Dzanga-Sangha Reserve. Outside these inner sanctums, carefully managed logging, hunting, and tourism activities may be allowed. Another such conservation area has been proposed in Cameroon.

Waterways offer access to Ndoki's tangled interior (above), but the riot of vegetation can quickly close off traffic. A raid on wild honey takes one of the Pygmies high above the ground (top); smoke dulls the bees protecting the hives. Ndoki's virgin trees reach more than 150 feet into the air.

FOLLOWING PAGES: Ndoki's thick forest dwarfs a researcher suspended by ropes in the canopy.

The problem with any activity near unspoiled areas lies not only with poaching but also with native people who have traditionally taken food from the bush. The easier it becomes to enter a game-rich area, the more likely they are to do so, despite official proclamations. To change such behavior, park officials are trying to educate local people about the value of leaving some of the forest sacrosanct. Some hunting is still allowed next to parklands, but wire snares that catch and mutilate large mammals are outlawed.

Villagers are being hired to build trails and structures for use by tourists, who will be allowed only at the peripheries of the parks and not into their inner sanctums. Former poachers are being trained as park guards, interpreters, and research assistants.

The new approach seems to be working. Some violators of the new rules have been turned in by their acquaintances. Villagers are learning that careful management of their wildlife will not only assure its future supply, but also provide an income from tourism. Conservationists are learning that much can be accomplished if the local people's well-being is also considered. And if Ndoki can be saved, the world can know that a truly wild sanctuary exists where man remains a stranger.

Shrinking Elephant Range

Although poaching for ivory was widely blamed for reducing the number of African elephants in the 1980s from 1.3 million to 608,000, an exploding human population gave them fewer places to hide. The ivory trade is now banned, but conflicts with people continue. More than 2 percent of Africa is set aside as parklands, but agriculture often pushes right up against park boundaries. An adult elephant eats 300 to 500 pounds of forage a day, and when elephants are crowded into too small a space they either destroy their own habitat or drift onto newly farmed land and eat the crops. Confronted by people they can become as aggressive as this charging forest elephant in Ndoki.

Shapers of forest, elephants cavort in an Ndoki water hole (opposite). Their bulk and big appetites create a network of trails and clearings used by many other animals. A lowland gorilla (left) wades a pool to reach food, the first photograph ever published of this animal in water.

Desert

*A*tacama, Mojave, Sahara, Kalahari, Gobi, Taklimakan. Names of grandeur declare the world's most inhospitable places. These are some of the harsh deserts that cover parts of all continents except Europe, in two wide belts, roughly at the tropics. The polar regions and many mountain summits are classified as deserts as well.

Deserts vary greatly, though all are marked, on average, by fewer than ten inches of rain a year, rapid evaporation, and sparse water. Feared for hot, unrelenting sun, they can become terribly cold at night as heat dissipates quickly into clear, cloudless skies.

The great Sahara of northern Africa, nearly the size of the United States, is a subtropical desert, maintained by climactic forces that keep rain away. West China's Taklimakan lies simply too far from large open water, and mountains block moisture-bearing clouds. Desiccated Patagonia suffers from a rain shadow; the tall Andean mass prevents wet Pacific air from reaching it. Southwest Africa's Namib falls in the class of cool coastal deserts, with virtually no rain. Only coastal fog and mist allow plants to exist. The polar regions are considered deserts, too, because precipitation is low and virtually all water remains trapped as ice.

Forces of erosion and deposition work on the land unceasingly. Wind, the constant winnower, separates particles, blowing some away, building different terrains, piling up dramatic duned deserts. Sands act as abrasives, cutting through the ages, creating such monuments as Utah's rock arches.

Desert surfaces, blisteringly hot, evaporate all liquid, but beneath, water percolates and remains. Many plants must find this hidden wetness to survive; some mesquite trees send down roots more than 250 feet.

Other flora use the tactic of dormancy. Seeds and leafless stems, quiescent for months or years, burst to life when rain arrives. These plants sometimes germinate and bloom within hours, and die a short time later after setting seed. The shallow fanlike roots of cactuses capture water quickly. Barrel and saguaro cactuses expand as they absorb available water, then shrink as the liquid is used up.

Animals have many desert tricks. Nocturnal rodents escape the worst of the sun, as do subterranean reptiles. Deer and antelope find liquid in succulent plants. A road runner, snake dangling from its mouth, soon refreshes itself with the blood and body juices of its prey. Camels obtain water through oxidation of fat in their humps. Foxes and hares sport elongated ears to aid heat loss, while among birds, the male sandgrouse has special water-absorbing feathers that

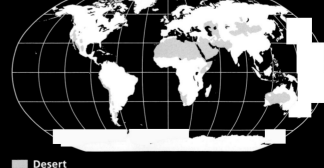

■ Desert

enable him to cool incubating eggs, and, later, quench hatchlings as they pass his wet feathers through their beaks.

Humans have not always been clever with the desert. Disastrous expansion of the Sahara into Sahel countries during the 1970s and 1980s resulted from overgrazing and overpopulation. Famine, death of livestock, and ecological degradation followed. Only care and planning can keep the deserts from growing: limit livestock, plant trees to cut wind and hardy grasses to stabilize sand, hold back the masses from marginal land.

Windswept dunes of the Namib, possibly the earth's oldest desert, shape the horizon. Long viewed as lifeless and forbidding, deserts around the world contain scenes of graceful beauty and serve as home to numerous creatures adapted to their harsh regimes.

Dense fog washes over dunes of Namibia's Skeleton Coast, bathing one of earth's most parched corners in moisture. The clouds leave droplets savored by the few hardy plants and animals. Riverbeds may be dry for years, although rains far inland feed a few underground seeps and springs.

Skeleton Coast

A place named for death and emptiness seems an unlikely location for a national park. The Skeleton Coast in southwest Africa adjoins what may be earth's oldest desert, the Namib, which translates from a local language as "where there is nothing." The macabre name of its coastline is derived from the remains of ships and whales that litter the sands. But the Skeleton Coast in Namibia is treasured for its stark beauty, and a surprising amount of life can be found there.

Portuguese discoverer Diego Cão found nothing but despair in its arid emptiness when he landed in 1486 after years of seeking a passage to India. He abandoned further exploration and died despondent on the voyage home. The arid shores were ignored by Europeans until the middle of the 19th century, when tons of bird guano were mined for fertilizer. A half century later it was found that gem-quality diamonds wash out of highlands to the east in flash floods sometimes years apart. Boom towns burgeoned, then went bust when the last easy fortunes were plucked from the sand and gravel. Today, a commercial operation mines deeper jewels.

The Benguela Current that has driven hundreds of ships to death on the shore has also breathed life on the land. The cold current flows northward along the coast, creating dangerous cross tides, heavy swells, and fog, a navigator's nightmare. Southwest sea breezes then push the dense fog inland 30 miles and more. Atmospheric pressure holds it low so it cannot rise and form rain clouds, but the fog delivers much-needed water to an area that may receive a half inch of rain annually. Since the Namib has been a desert some 55 million years, plants and animals have developed ingenious ways of drinking from the murk.

Two species of dwarf shrubs have leaves that sift moisture from the fog. A tall dune grass sends out shallow roots more than 60 feet to soak up droplets from the surface of the sand. The welwitschia plant, sometimes thousands of years old, grows two long leaves with countless pores that absorb deposited moisture, and also sends a root 20 feet deep to tap

underground water. The naras plant grows deep roots and produces a melon-like fruit eaten by jackals, gerbils, lizards, and beetles.

To escape heat and find food, some reptiles and insects live on the surface as well as just under the loose sands on the slip faces of the tallest dunes in the world, blown to sculpted crescents up to a thousand feet high. A totally sightless golden mole also swims through the sand, hunting geckos, crickets, and beetle larvae. The darkling beetle practically stands on its head when the fog rolls in, letting moisture slide down its back toward its mouth parts. Snakes and lizards lick condensation off their scales.

Even large mammals manage to survive in this driest land. Giraffes eat leaves glistening with dew. Elephants go days without a drink while journeying from one rare oasis to another. In dry riverbeds they dig holes to let water seep in. The gemsbok antelope has a network of capillaries in its nose that cools its blood before it reaches the brain. Lions once preyed on them and on the thousands of Cape fur seals that come ashore. The lions have disappeared within the past decade, some driven off by drought, others shot by herdsmen who also live in the Namib and fear for their livestock. Seabirds are plentiful on the shore, drawn by the fecund marine life in the nutrient-rich cold current.

In 1971 a 300-mile sliver of the coast, no more than 25 miles wide, was declared the Skeleton Coast Park by Namibia. While hunting is forbidden, many large animals become vulnerable when they drift outside its boundaries, although new reserves adjoining the park may offer protection. The elephant population was reduced from 300 to about 70 by hunters and drought in the 1980s, but their numbers are climbing again now that stronger antipoaching measures are in place. Recognizing the income available from tourism, the Namibian government has increased its protection of the park. Tourist income is shared with villagers, and locals have been hired as game guards. The barren coast has become popular with ecotourists who come to enjoy the solitude that this "land of nothing" has always offered.

A harsh land of soft curves and strange contrasts, the Skeleton Coast's rich sea border draws hosts of aquatic animals to the edge of aridity. Cold water upwellings bring nutrients that attract marine life and those that feed on it. Near a sinuous sand dune, flamingos stalk a productive lagoon (opposite). When not pursuing fish, Cape fur seals (above) come ashore by the thousand. Long ignored as a land of death and emptiness, the coast is now visited by tourists fascinated by its stark charms.

FOLLOWING PAGES: The graveyard for ships claims another victim. Often wrecked in dense fog on unexpected shoals, the bones of lost boats contributed to the Skeleton Coast's macabre name.

AFRICA

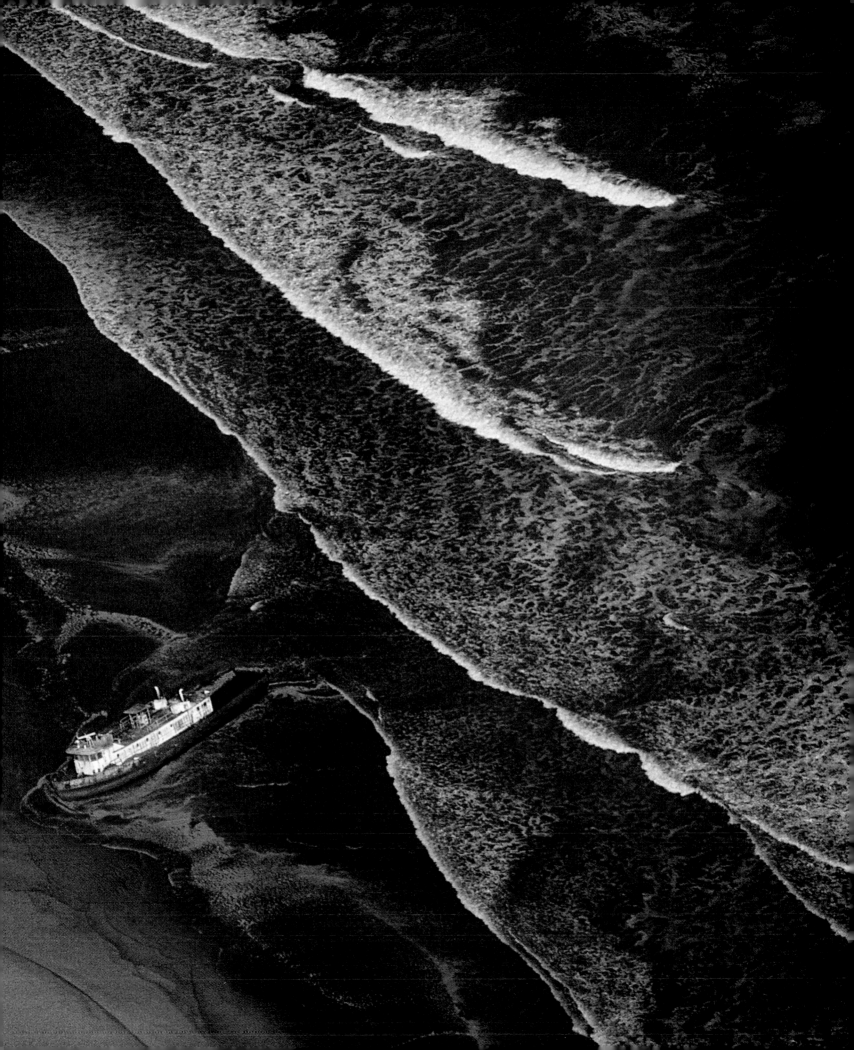

Virungas

round A.D. 150, Ptolemy suggested that the Nile originated in a legendary African range he called the "Mountains of the Moon." No one knows exactly how the early geographer came up with that name, as he had never laid eyes on the volcanic range. But if Ptolemy somehow sensed the mystery of the high spine at the western edge of the Great Rift Valley, he was right on target. The Virunga Mountains and the towering Ruwenzori with their unusual plants and animals eluded explorers nearly two millennia, then became Africa's first national park early in this century. Today, Zaire's Virunga National Park is home to some of the last mountain gorillas.

The gentle giants, some weighing 400 pounds, are a huskier version of the more plentiful lowland gorillas. They had been identified as a separate species for less than 20 years when American naturalist Carl Akeley realized in 1921 that trophy hunters were wiping them out. The Mountains of the Moon were then part of the vast Belgian Congo. Akeley petitioned for protection of the gorillas, and in 1925 King Albert of Belgium set aside the heart of the Virungas as Albert National Park. Within four years it expanded to include half a million acres of the Virungas, the Ruindi and Rutshuru Plains, and the Ruwenzoris.

When Zaire gained its independence, the area was renamed Virunga National Park. The creation of new international boundaries through the mountains provided added protection in three parks, all connected: Virunga in Zaire, Ruwenzori National Park on the Uganda side of the tallest mountains, and Volcanoes National Park in Rwanda. The latter became famous as the site of Karisoke, researcher Dian Fossey's wilderness camp where she worked to save mountain gorillas before being mysteriously killed in 1985.

The protected areas present a layer cake of ecosystems, from baking plains to glaciers, all virtually on the Equator. Grazing on the grasses of the low savanna are cape buffalo, kob antelope, and the topi antelope sporting purplish spots on their reddish brown flanks as though they had lain in ink. Hippos oink in pools, and lions pant in the shade by day and hunt at night. Elephants, well protected here during years of intense ivory hunting, carry large tusks.

On the slopes the rain forest takes over, rampant with ferns, vines, blackberry, and wild celery, a gorilla smorgasbord. The air grows cooler,

In mountains long protected by thick vegetation, giant heather trees in the Virungas of Zaire cast bizarre shapes against a morning sky. Legendary but unpeopled for hundreds of years, these jungled, sawtooth peaks harbor some of the world's last mountain gorillas, threatened by regional civil war.

Scenes of quiet beauty abound high in the Ruwenzori, known along with the Virungas as the "Mountains of the Moon" by ancient Greeks. More than 200 inches of rain a year feed oversize plants like these groundsels (below), taller than a man. Lower savannas are home to the crowned crane (right), one of the continent's loveliest birds.

Virungas

frequent showers are chilly, and the gorillas need their thick hair. Higher on the mountains little duiker antelope dart furtively amid bright green bamboo forests, hunted by leopards. On the Ruwenzori the bamboo gives way to thick mosses and twisted, dwarfed conifers stunted by the thin air, their branches laced with dollar-green lichens. An earthworm a yard long slithers through the moss carpet kept soggy by more than 200 inches of rain a year. Above tree line grows a band of bizarre plants, oversize lobelia spikes stabbing 20 feet in the air, and heather 40 feet tall. Groundsels that a gardener

might stoop to examine elsewhere tower over a man's head. Near the alpine peaks of the Ruwenzori—6 of them over 16,000 feet—lives the rock hyrax, rabbit-size and groundhog-shaped, but related to the elephant.

Each of these mountain layers can be extremely peaceful, but pressures against the lower ground persist. Rwanda is one of the most densely populated countries in Africa, and the search for firewood and game often disrupts the peaceful existence of the gorillas in Volcanoes National Park. Poachers stalk them, seeking to sell gorilla infants as pets and adult body parts as oddities. Civil unrest in recent years has resulted in some gorilla deaths from gunfire and perhaps a land mine, and refugees in temporary camps have destroyed gorilla habitat.

With the losses have come positive signs. Income from wildlife tourism had become so important that the Zairian owner of one tourism company hires his own commandos to battle poachers. Rwandan guards stayed behind and tried to protect Karisoke even after it was officially evacuated and their salaries had ceased. Despite the loss of some gorillas, the majority survived and efforts to protect them continue. Education programs urge local citizens to value their wildlife and if peace can be sustained, the Mountains of the Moon may dazzle visitors for years to come.

Politics and Preservation

When political power is at stake, the survival of an animal species takes a back seat, especially to combatants who have little appreciation for the values of preservation. In Rwanda's four-year civil war, one gorilla was caught in a crossfire in Rwanda. Four others were shot in Zaire, and another may have been killed when it stepped on a land mine. Gorilla habitat was destroyed when refugees in huge camps collected firewood and bamboo for mats and blankets from the forest. Park guards (below) heroically stayed at their posts during the war to prevent poaching. At the war's end, the losing army retreating through Volcanoes National Park angrily ransacked Dian Fossey's Karisoke camp.

Virungas

Burly survivor of poaching and war, a 21-year-old gorilla named Titus forages in a giant senecio *tree* in Rwanda's Volcanoes National Park. Near here the late Dian Fossey set up the Karisoke Research Center, where her studies of the gentle mountain gorillas belied their ferocious reputation. Her camp, sacked and abandoned in a recent conflict, is now being repaired, Despite her efforts, gorillas like this reclusive youngster (below) are still eye to eye with extinction.

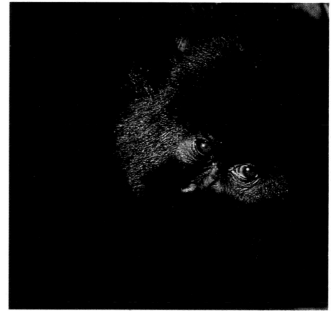

Grasslands

f the savannas and grasslands were theater, we would say they lacked box office appeal. They don't offer the grandeur of the mountains, the mystery of forests, or the power and mood of the seas. Perhaps no habitat is so underappreciated. Grasslands cover nearly a third of the earth's land surface, and before human influence they sustained enormous herds of mammals. The weight of bison on the North American plains once exceeded the weight of all people now living on the continent. Where converted to crops, grasslands now supply three-quarters of the world's energy needs. Indirectly, they supply even more food by providing forage for the animals we consume.

In their natural states they may be the most efficient of habitats. An African savanna produces four and a half pounds of plant matter per square yard of soil each year, half the weight produced by a rain forest. But that weight is attained with a tenth of the biomass produced by the rain forest. And the energy is edible and therefore recycled quickly, not locked up for years in a long-lived tree.

Temperate grasslands occur in areas that are too dry for forests but not dry enough to become desert. Flames ignited by lightning or indigenous peoples and sweeping over the American Great Plains destroyed shrubs and trees. Savannas are grasslands found at tropical latitudes where long dry seasons and thin soils prevent rain forest from becoming established. Where scattered trees do occur in a grassland they provide shade for mammals and nesting areas for birds. They also enrich the species mix by providing food for those that prefer tree foliage over grass.

The differing diets of herbivores enhance the plains. In the Serengeti, zebra graze on the rough, tallest part of the grasses, followed by wildebeest, which crop the shorter grass that the zebra have exposed. Gazelles then nip the tender new shoots that spring up in the wildebeest's wake. A survey showed that areas not grazed at all declined in the quality and quantity of their forage.

Grassland residents vary around the globe, but no areas reached the huge concentrations of Africa and North America. The llanos of South America between the Andes and the Orinoco River flood during the rainy season, eliminating burrowing plant eaters and large hoofed animals. The soggy conditions are perfect, however, for the capybara, a pig-size rodent that is equally at home in the water or on land. Marsupials—kangaroos and wallabies—are the native trimmers of the grasslands that cover large stretches of

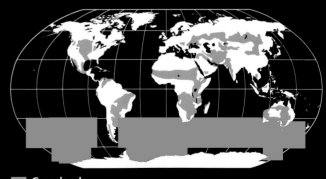

■ Grasslands

Australia. Similar to the pronghorn of North America, the swift saiga of the Eurasian steppes survives winter's fierce storms by a brutal selection process. After mating, some four-fifths of the males starve themselves, leaving food for the females bearing the young.

By such strategies have the grasslands and their creatures sustained themselves. The biggest consumers now are humans whose food demands have turned great plains into croplands. Productive though they may be, the conversions alter ecosystems balanced over millions of years.

Belly deep in grazing, zebras and wildebeests relax in Kenya's Masai Mara. Both frequent open savannas and migrate together with the seasons in search of ample food and water.

Their thundering hordes demonstrate the life-sustaining efficiency of the world's grasslands.

Serengeti

The vast plain in Tanzania and Kenya filled with the most extravagant hordes of hoofed animals on the continent includes probably the most famous wildlife sanctuary in the world—Serengeti National Park in Tanzania. Unmatched herds of grazers sometimes extend to the horizon and their sinuous predators are plentiful. Visitors feel transported to the dawn of time.

This immense wilderness emerged with the splitting of tectonic plates more than 35 million years ago that created the Great Rift Valley system. The plains were then covered with wind-blown ash from extensive volcanism, leaving fertile soil for grass but forming compactions not far beneath the surface that discouraged tree growth in some areas.

For centuries the animal populations had the Serengeti virtually to themselves, as they established natural rhythms of reproduction and predation. Masai moved down from the north and into the valley little more than a century ago, but made little impact with their modest herds of cattle. The valley name comes from the Masai word *siringet,* or "endless plains." Although scattered trees stud much of the Serengeti and woodlands can be found in the north and west, the flattest of the grasslands sometimes stretch uninterrupted for 40 to 50 miles. Professional hunters from Europe discovered this wildlife cornucopia in 1913 and began shooting game with abandon. Lions were plentiful and considered vermin, and safaris bagging a hundred were not uncommon. These largest predators were reduced so drastically that to protect them and other species the area was declared a full game reserve in 1929. In 1951, with conservation movements spreading around the globe, the Serengeti became a national park. Today, its boundaries encompass 5,700 square miles, roughly the size of Connecticut, but the entire Serengeti-Mara ecosystem is about twice that size. It extends north to Kenya's Masai Mara reserve, south to the volcanic Ngorongoro. Conservation Area, east into the Loliondo Highlands, and west to the shores of Lake Victoria.

This extended Serengeti is defined by the annual migrations of the wildebeest, the most plentiful of the large animals in the park. When the short grasslands of the southeast dry up around May, the strange-looking antelope begin moving west, honking, snorting, bucking, and breeding on their way to the floodplains of Lake Victoria in columns up to 25 miles long.

A world of its own, the Serengeti reflects an earlier epoch when animals dominated plains everywhere. On grasslands often covered by multitudes of grazers, two impalas stand silhouetted against a setting sun.

FOLLOWING PAGES: A sea of horns and stripes mills over the Masai Mara at the northern edge of the Serengeti ecosystem. Never far from water, both follow the rains over the 10,000 square miles of the Serengeti, about half of which receives protection as parklands.

Families of zebra float within the ocean of brown like bright flotsam. Some gazelles drift along partway, but the less far-ranging buffalo, giraffe, waterbuck, and topi tend to stay on familiar ground. The tiny dik-dik, an antelope the size of a large house cat, may never leave its home acre.

When the plains of the west wither as the dry season (between June and October) becomes more intense, the wildebeests move to permanent rivers in the north and northeast. When they've mown the grass short and the females are about to calve, they move back to the wide-open plains of the southeast as the rains resume, having completed a triangular migration that lasted nearly nine months.

The extravaganza annually draws some 15,000 human visitors to the Serengeti. Six luxury lodges and numerous campsites are within park boundaries. A pride of lions resting on the island-like kopjes, mounds of smooth-topped granite that dot the plains, may be surrounded by a dozen vehicles.

Visitors must be prepared for viewing life at its most basic. This is a land of the quick and the dead, and on the open grasslands it is often highly visible. An army of predators lurks at the fringes of the herds, looking for weaknesses. Lions stalk to take prey in a final rush, or lie in wait at water holes. Packs of wild dogs looking for the weak and the undefended pull down victims in seven out of ten attempts. Hyenas specialize in young calves. In the lemming-like migrations the wildebeests pile up in rivers and hundreds drown, feeding crocodiles and vultures. Annual losses of the bearded, clownlike beasts with their long faces and crescent-shaped horns may be as much as 50 percent. Barring unusual drought they manage to replenish themselves year after year. They in turn regulate the numbers of their regulators; in lean times when the wildebeests move elsewhere, those of fang and claw must hunt more scattered prey. Many predators do not survive. Hyenas eat lion cubs, eagles eat hyena pups, and lions kill adult hyenas whenever they can.

Wildebeests dominate, but there are many other players in this drama. Impalas leap in soaring arcs, ostriches race across the plains, and there are hippopotamuses, baboons, vervet monkeys, and some 450 species of birds. Sleek cheetahs run down gazelles and young wildebeests at speeds of 60 miles an hour. Leopards leap from ambush, and from tree limbs where they drape their lithe bodies in repose.

The land of the quick and the dead includes the world's fastest runner, the cheetah (opposite), resting protectively over her cub. But the speed of parents cannot save young cheetahs that run afoul of lions like this pride resting under a stormy sky (above). Among the Serengeti's most efficient predators are wild dogs, here pulling down a doomed wildebeest. Seven out of ten hunts by the canines end in success.

The Enchanted Chalice

More than two million years ago the volcano Ngorongoro had built a cone 15,000 feet high before a final violent eruption blew off the top. Dozens of cubic miles of magma were blasted out followed by fine ash, leaving the giant underground cavity the mountain collapsed into when the eruption ceased. Some 2,000 feet of the mountain's outer walls remained, cupping a 100-square-mile floor of what is now the world's largest caldera. Eventually grass covered the floor and seepage provided a water supply to the natural amphitheater, attracting elephants, hippos, rhinos, zebras, wildebeests, gazelles, buffaloes, ostriches, and warthogs, and predators such as lions, hyenas, jackals, and foxes.

The first human visitors reported no elephants in the Serengeti, but expanding human populations elsewhere drove them here about mid-century. Browsing elephants have created more grassland by smashing down northern woodlands to eat foliage. Elephants were driven into the park by farming pressures, and in the 1980s were severely poached in northern sections of the park—scattering the herds. Greatest poaching losses have been to the black rhino, taken illegally for the horn that many Asians believe has medicinal powers. Rhino populations in the Serengeti plunged in a decade from about 500 to less than 20, and continent-wide they are considered near extinction.

Smaller ungulates fall illegally to local hunters seeking meat for the pot. High human population growth poses a more serious threat. Motorized operations now poach large amounts of game for a profitable commercial market. Improved medical and veterinary health have also increased the numbers of cattle in the area, which compete with wildlife for the grass. The Masai continue to pressure for more grazing land for their livestock.

In the mid-1990s more evidence of human crowding surfaced when lions in the park began dying of distemper, picked up from domestic dogs living at the edge of the park. A third of the population of some 3,000 were lost before survivors developed an immunity to the disease, but researchers fear a recurrence by more virulent strains. A fund has been created to vaccinate villagers' dogs against distemper and rabies.

The sheer numbers of wild animals in the Serengeti ecosystem work

in their favor. Critical to survival of the all-important wildebeest is the maintenance of its huge, triangular migration route. As long as host governments remain receptive to tourist dollars and the animals are given a reasonable chance to regulate themselves, this sweeping landscape and its cast of millions will remain one of the most amazing wildlife spectacles in the world.

Pod of gold impalas appears at rainbow's end in Masai Mara. Unlike other herbivores, impalas do not migrate with the rain but switch from grazing to browsing in the dry season. Renowned jumpers, they add grace to the plains of the Serengeti, the world's greatest wildlife spectacle.

Other Wild Places

BLOOMING ALOE PLANT, MADAGASCAR

Air and Ténéré National Nature Reserve

Niger Rare animal species and an increasingly rare way of life are being protected in this arid reserve covering nearly 30,000 square miles, roughly 6 percent of Niger's total area. Habitats include the shifting sands of the Ténéré Desert with temperatures that range from 122°F in summer to below zero in winter. In the humid Air Mountains dense mists condense on cold nights into pools of ground water. These are some of the last refuges for wildlife that once ranged over much of the Sahara and Sahel. Protected are the endangered addax, an antelope weighing more than 200 pounds, and the oryx with its scimitar-shaped horns. Reclusive Barbary sheep, actually a kind of mountain goat, live at high altitudes. Cheetahs, jackals, hyenas, ostriches, and various

CHAMELEON CROSSING THE KALAHARI DESERT

gazelles can also be found.

Some 3,000 people, mostly semi-nomadic conservation-minded Tuaregs, live in the reserve, raising camels and goats, tending gardens for food, and hunting. The reserve's planners hope that by educating newcomers to the dangers of overgrazing and overhunting, the region will serve as a model of integrating conservation with preserving the lifestyles of a local population.

Gashaka Gumti Reserve

Nigeria The nation with the largest population in Africa would seem to have few hidden corners left, but Nigeria's largest protected area has some parts that are yet unknown to biologists. Gashaka Gumti Reserve, nearly 4,000 square miles in the remote southeast corner of oil-rich Nigeria, contains savanna, rain forest, and uplands that are home to some endangered species. Leopards and rare golden cats prey on abundant antelope, gazelles, wildebeests, and hartebeests. Among the eight types of primates, endangered mountain gorillas may live on forested slopes so remote they have not yet been explored. Reserve managers are trying to balance the needs of a local native population with wildlife protection. The Nigerian government hopes to promote ecotourism by facilitating wildlife viewing in the little-known area.

Bale Mountains National Park

Ethiopia Tectonic activity deep within the earth pushed up the Ethiopian Highlands millions of years ago, then set apart the Bale Mountains by opening the Great Rift Valley. The result was the largest area of high ground in all Africa, at least 400 square miles standing above 11,000 feet. The rising of the dome like a giant soufflé also created cracks in its surface, visible today as deep valleys between the mountain blocks. The variety of habitats includes tropical forest in the southern lowlands, rising to mountain woods and grasslands, well-watered moorland on higher slopes, and the high, windswept Sanetti Plateau at the top.

Ranging through the northern woodlands and grasslands is the mountain nyala, a kind of antelope with horns that begin to arc over its back before curling forward in a question mark. The damp chill of high, tundra slopes has discouraged human habitation, and isolation has protected a number of species known only to Ethiopia. Simien jackals live in close-knit packs in which all members provide food for the pups and guard them against birds of prey. The jackals' main prey is the giant mole rat, a rodent weighing more than two pounds that burrows in the moorlands. The mountains have their own species of hare called Stark's hare and a unique bird called Rouget's rail.

Madagascar

This island of unique plants and creatures is often referred to as the land that time forgot. Separated from the African mainland some 165 million years ago, its flora and fauna evolved differently from all others. All the lemurs in the world and half its chameleon species are found here. Of its 10,000 known species of flowering plants, well over half of them are endemic to Madagascar. It is a land of hissing cockroaches and primates with goblin eyes.

The planet's fourth largest island—976 miles long by 354 wide—is nearly a miniature continent with varying climates and ecosystems. Trade winds from the Indian Ocean drop substantial rainfall on the northeast coast, nurturing tropical forests where four-fifths of the plants are found nowhere else. A ridge of mountains blocks moisture from the southwest coast, resulting in a desert where spiny succulents grow that bear no relation to cactus. The central highlands are temperate.

Madagascar's odd species have suffered greatly from slash-and-burn agriculture and logging. Only 20 percent of the original forest cover remains. Rural families are now offered training, tools, seeds, schools, and improved water supplies if they will stop cutting trees. Tourism is seen as a means of income and preservation of endangered species, but the island is underequipped for handling visitors.

Tassili-n-Ajjer National Park

Algeria The Sahara Desert may seem an unlikely place for a national park, but this dusty plateau in southeastern Algeria contains what one scholar called "the largest open-air museum in the world." The plateau rises from the desert in a fortresslike wall nearly 2,000 feet high and covers 30,000 square miles. The raised land is cut and ribbed by rains of long ago, from a time when Tassili-n-Ajjer bloomed with life, and from a later time when dry winds carved more shapes in the terrain. In the walls of the deep ravines and canyons thousands of paintings and engravings document a more verdant past.

While Europe was wrapped in glaciers, lime and olive trees bloomed in Tassili-n-Ajjer and around pools and

MOUNT KILIMANJARO

waterfalls oaks, oleanders, and myrtle thrived. Both wild and domestic animals browsed in abundance. In a history lesson written in stone, rock paintings show the passage by earlier people from hunting and gathering to primitive agriculture and cattle raising. As the climate changed, depictions of cattle and horses gave way to sketches of oryx, gazelles, ostriches, and camels. Eventually nothing was left on the plateau but stone fences, shards of pottery, and spear points, and the marvelous frescoes for today's tourists to contemplate.

Kalahari Desert

Botswana The Kalahari Desert covers more than 80 percent of Botswana. It is a part-time desert, watered for five months from October to March and dry for most of the remainder of the year. In the damp periods when vegetation flourishes and water gathers in shallow pans, wildlife flocks to the vast 100,400-square-mile plateau. Precipitation varies from north to south, as does the wildlife. Rainfall averages 18 inches a year, too slight to support agriculture, but a few scattered herders and occasional bushmen live in the vast expanse of the Kalahari.

Off the few driving roads in the vastness lies an Africa unspoiled by humans. Woodlands cover the north where heavier rains, 25 inches annually, support both deciduous and coniferous trees, and rich animal life. Large herds of elephants live along the border with Zimbabwe to the east and the Caprivi Strip to the west, along with giraffes, zebras, antelopes, and buffaloes, and predators such as lions, cheetahs, leopards, wild dogs, and hyenas.

Even in the arid south where the rains dwindle to five inches a year, wildebeest, hartebeest, eland, kudu, and duiker drift onto the plains during the rainy season. Where water soaks too quickly into the porous soil, some of the animals obtain moisture from eating fruit. The predators—cheetahs, lions, jackals, and hyenas—follow the ungulates like shadows.

Mount Kilimanjaro

Tanzania This almost perfectly formed volcanic cone in Tanzania is the highest peak in all Africa and probably the most beautiful. A relative newcomer, the volcano began erupting about 750,000 years ago and stopped major activity about 400,000 years later, although Kibo, one of the three peaks, may have erupted within the past few hundred years.

Snowcapped with emerald rain forest creeping up its lower slopes, it annually attracts some 15,000 visitors to the Mount Kilimanjaro National Park. Not all who attempt the climb reach the summit, at 19,340 feet. An arduous five-day walk is required, but climbers have included a youngster of 11 and an oldster of 74. The mountain can be climbed anytime, but rain is plentiful during April, May, and November, and the huts on the way up are usually fully booked around Christmas and the New Year. The climb can be undertaken independently, but several outfitters rent camping gear and offer guides and porters who carry equipment and fix meals, and the savings of not using them is minimal. In the space of a few days a climber can ascend from rain forest through moorland, alpine desert, and finally snow and ice. Altitude sickness is common, but the final assault is made in predawn hours and sunrise at the top is spectacular.

PANGOLIN, CENTRAL AFRICA

ICELAND

ATLANTIC OCEAN

Cairngorm
Mountains

North
Sea

IRELAND

UNITED
KINGDOM

NORWAY

Hardangervidda
National
Park

SWEDEN

FINLAND

DENMARK

Baltic Sea

RUSSIA

ESTONIA

LATVIA

LITHUANIA

RUSSIA

BELARUS

Don

Elbe

NETH.

BELG.

GERMANY

POLAND

Białowieża
National Park

UKRAINE

Seine

LUX.

FRANCE

Rhine

LIECH.

SWITZ.

Vanoise
National Park

A L P S

Gran Paradiso
National
Park

Hohe Tauern
N.P.

AUSTRIA

CZECH. REP.

High Tatra N.P.

Tatra National Park

SLOVAKIA

Dnieper

MOLDOVA

HUNGARY

SLOV.

CROATIA

BOSN. &
HERZG.

YUG.

ROMANIA

Black
Sea

BULGARIA

TURKEY

PORTUGAL

SPAIN

ANDORRA

ITALY

ALBANIA

MACED.

GREECE

Sardinia

Gennargentu
Mountains

Vikos
Gorge

Huelva

Seville

Doñana National
Park

Strait of
Gibraltar

Mediterranean

Sea

MALTA

0   300 Mi
0   500 Km

Europe

by Elisabeth B. Booz

A visitor to modern, industrialized Europe might well assume that any trace of wilderness had vanished centuries ago. But in fact, thousands of protected nature reserves and national parks enliven Europe's 40-odd countries; they range in size from mountain chains and river deltas to a single rock in the North Sea where gannets nest.

Unlike the United States, which conceived the idea of national parks with immense tracts of wilderness, Europe could only gather up the bits of land that were left after centuries of civilization, wars, and shifting national boundaries. Astonishingly, many wild places survived. Some of these were too inaccessible to be useful, like rugged mountains, or too hard to farm, like salt marshes. Better yet were wild, often forested areas that kings and nobles saved as hunting preserves. After World War I, some of these lands became public trusts, overseen by governments and scientists. Italy and Poland were able to use natural habitats on former royal domains to bring back ibex and bison from the brink of extinction.

In today's Europe the desire of more and more people to visit beautiful, unspoiled, wild places often collides with the original purpose of protecting wilderness from disruption by human activities. Where ecologists and others have influenced governments, natural areas have usually been carefully managed for study, education, enjoyment, and outdoor sports.

A more insidious threat to nature is the pollution of Europe's air and waters. Hope lies in the emerging European Union, which shows signs of giving the environment top priority. If it can enforce draconian rules on its members' industries, it may one day finance a system of well-protected European parks to benefit a whole continent of nature lovers.

Volga

Caspian Sea

KAZAKSTAN

Astrakhan
State
Nature
Reserve

Volga
River
Delta

Cairngorms

My heart's in the Highlands, my heart is not here,
My heart's in the Highlands a-chasing the deer.

Poet Robert Burns might well have been thinking of the Cairngorm Mountains in northeast Scotland when he wrote those lines around 1790. Heather still turns the steep mountainsides purple in August, and the red deer still runs free. Nature lovers and conservationists want to keep the area wild forever.

The high hollow corries of these mountains stay white well into the summer. Winter blizzards wrap the 4,000-foot Cairngorm Mountains in more snow than any other uplands in Britain, creating an exotic patch of Arctic wilderness in the heart of the Highlands. None but the hardiest plants or birds survive on the weathered domes.

The Cairngorms, bounded by the rivers Dee and Spey, form Britain's largest discrete mountain region, covering some 400 square miles. Ice Age glaciers shaped the Cairngorms, gouging basinlike corries and steep-sided glens from a lofty granite plateau. Icy streams brought down sands and gravel to form the harsh soil of the Old Caledonian Forest that eventually covered a large part of Scotland. Scots pines, relicts of the primeval forest, still fill the narrow valleys.

In 1954 the British government selected more than a hundred square miles as a national nature reserve for its extraordinary concentration of geological features, habitats and species. The wooded glens offer refuge in heavily populated Britain for a variety of mammals, birds, and insects. Rare crested tits and endemic Scottish crossbills nest in the pines, while the small red squirrels that have almost vanished from England feast on pine nuts. Wild cats and pine martens prowl in the underbrush, and the Cairngorms' rivers, marshes, and lochs are home to otters and ospreys. In spring, a proud male capercaillie, a rare, turkeylike grouse with scarlet eye-patches, may command the forest floor with its courtship dance.

Rugged plants hug the heathered slopes above, their woolly or waxen leaves adapted to the icy wind. Rare species such as Highland saxifrage and hare's foot sedge find shelter in circular corries. Young heather shoots attract timid mountain hares, though the open ground poses danger from golden

Still waters of Loch an Eilein reflect ancient pinewoods in the Scottish Highlands. The wild Cairngorm Mountains shelter a variety of mammals, birds, and insects that have vanished from other parts of the country. National nature reserves help keep the wilderness from overuse by tourists and skiers.

eagles and peregrine falcons nesting in the high crags. Higher yet, white winter plumage keeps the feather-footed ptarmigan invisible in the snow, and a flock of white-winged snow buntings, dipping and turning in flight, can be mistaken for a sudden snow flurry.

Undisputed monarchs of the forests and moors are the handsome red deer, their stags crowned with regal antlers. In summer, separate herds of stags and hinds climb the slopes to eat shrubs and grasses and escape the troublesome, biting flies below. But in winter they descend to become the scourge of the forest. Returning to the glens, the herds feed for months on tender pine seedlings, the forest's future. As the great virgin pines grow old there is little new growth to replace them.

Other deer share the same habitat and contribute to the damage. Smaller roe deer in family groups feed on shrubs. A few reindeer forage for mosses and lichens on the high plateaus. Like their extinct ancestors, reindeer have acclimated easily into the Cairngorms' wilderness after being reintroduced from Sweden in 1952. But the red deer dominate in both size and numbers.

The greatest threats to the Cairngorms' ecosystem

come from red deer and humans. Both have proved difficult to control. Though the forest is dying, owners of profitable hunting estates within and adjacent to the nature reserve traditionally opposed the much-needed culling of deer. Recently, the need to regenerate the Caledonian forest has gained recognition and support.

Nature lovers, hikers, and sportsmen have always enjoyed the remote Cairngorms. The number of visitors to the region increased dramatically in the 1960s, when a ski area with a chairlift opened on Cairn Gorm. Thirty years later, developers eager for year-round tourism clashed with conservation groups—including the Royal Society for the Protection of Birds which owns a 32,000-acre bird reserve in the Cairngorms. A new plan proposes a funicular railway to replace the chairlift, and an educational visitor's center just below Cairn Gorm's summit. But talk of limiting visitors to ranger-led nature walks infuriates traditional hikers. Walkers, rock climbers, naturalists, commercial interests, planners, and landowners are wrestling with conflicts and problems that are proving hard to resolve.

Regal red deer hinds survey their domain (opposite, above). Now numerous, stags and hinds form separate herds during most of the year. Their winter diet of pine seedlings prevents natural regeneration of the primeval forest. A female black grouse (opposite, below) feeds on pine scrub at the forest edge. Ancient Scots pines (below) survive from the Old Caledonian Forest that once covered much of Scotland. Slabs of rough bark are a protective adaptation against bark-stripping by browsing deer.

A distant flock of birds greets the dawn over Doñana National Park. Marshlands, upland scrub, and dunes form three distinct ecosystems in one of Europe's last great wildernesses. Conservationists, Spanish farmers, and real estate developers argue fiercely over the use of Doñana's limited water resources.

Doñana

Atlantic breakers surge against an empty, sandy shore. No beach boardwalk or food concession interrupts a 15-mile sweep on Spain's south coast. No sounds intrude save the cry of a gull and the muted hubbub of hundreds of thousands of birds massed in the salt marshes stretching back beyond the beach. Overhead, an eagle glides over a vast, flat scrubland, scanning for furry prey. Three distinct landscapes—dunes, marshland, and scrub—exist side by side and interact in natural harmony at Doñana National Park. The park's 195 square miles form one of Western Europe's largest and most diversified wildernesses.

Doñana, as it is known in Spain, faces the Atlantic Ocean at the mouth of Andalusia's broad Guadalquivir River. For travelers, roads link the park with the cities of Seville and Huelva. For migrating birds, flyways link it to Europe and Africa at a point near the Strait of Gibraltar. In spring, nearly half of all Europe's migratory bird species rest and feed in Doñana's marshes, breaking the long flight from Africa to their home nesting sites.

Most of the multitude continue their flight before summer drought turns the wetland into cracked, gray-green mudflats. Some birds remain. Rare purple gallinules breed in reed beds; storks and spoonbills nest in the tops of gnarled cork oaks; and some 30 Spanish imperial eagles, defying extinction, claim lordship over the pinewoods, ponds, and scrubland.

An ever growing sandbar separates Doñana from the sea. White Sahara-like dunes conceal haunts of the short-toed eagle and the reptiles it preys upon. Green pinewoods in the swales and gray skeletons of trees half buried in sand tell a story of ever shifting, advancing dunes. Inland, shallow lagoons and forests of stone pine and cork oak form a rich habitat between the sands and the scrubland. Large animals such as wild boar and the rare Iberian lynx dwell in the woods while red and fallow deer hide in the scrub that extends to the edge of the marshes.

Though far outnumbered by birds, mammals kept Doñana wild for 500 years as a royal game preserve. King Alfonso XI of Spain commented on the plentiful boar around 1345. After the seventh duke of Medina-Sidonia acquired the land in 1585, his reclusive duchess, Doña Ana, occupied a small palace on the hunting estate. Her name was given to the area, and contracted to Doñana.

Stately flamingos stalk through Doñana's vast salt marshes searching for shrimp (above) or fly overhead in pink-winged elegance (opposite, below) during seasonal visits to the strategically located wetlands. Nearly half of all Europe's bird species visit Doñana each year, finding rest and food at a vital crossroads of African and European migration routes. Countless water-fowl and other birds stay to breed during spring and summer.

Pristine sandy beaches arc for 15 miles on the Atlantic Ocean near Gibraltar, free from development (opposite, above). Dunes stretch inland toward lakes and green pinewoods, which, in turn, merge into higher scrub and vast expanses of marshland (opposite, below).

Europeans learned about Doñana's birdlife around 1910 from the writings of Abel Chapman, a traveling English naturalist. By the 1950s scientists had recognized the area's crucial role for migrating birds and many species of vanishing wildlife. When the Spanish government proposed draining Doñana for rice cultivation, the World Wildlife Fund helped Spanish ecologists buy 29 square miles of the wilderness for a biological reserve. In 1969 the government established the area as Doñana National Park and gradually increased its size with protective buffer zones. Today, Doñana's administrators protect the park by limiting visitors to 250 a day. Camping and hiking are forbidden. Guards patrol against poachers.

Conflicts with the local population multiplied as agriculture and tourism developed on the park's periphery. Water usage by hotels and villas, and thirsty crops such as rice and strawberries have measurably lowered Doñana's water table. Prohibited pesticides seeping into the marshes from neighboring fields killed some 30,000 waterfowl in 1986. The culprits were never identified. A nearby seaside town planned a large summer tourist resort—for the very season when water is scarcest. But, not unreasonably, the inhabitants of this impoverished region seek to

Doñana

share in Spain's growing prosperity.

In 1990 the Spanish government responded to international outcry by halting highway construction and a new irrigation project near the park. Andalusia's regional government commissioned a team of international experts to study Doñana's problems. Their report in 1992 advised a vigorous combination of conservation and economic development. Their plan called for greatly expanded, high-quality ecotourism, which would provide local employment. Strict water regulations and help in marketing were proposed as ways of persuading farmers to grow ecologically beneficial crops. The report recommended that an enlarged area be renamed Doñana European Park, with an international center for environmental studies, but as yet there are no plans for implementing what could become a model for other European natural reserves.

FOLLOWING PAGES: Shadows of stone pines dapple the white sand of Doñana's dunes. Windblown sand spilling from their crests keeps the dunes moving inland as the sandbar grows. Tree-filled corrales, or swales, shelter a variety of wildlife, such as the endangered Iberian lynx.

Gran Paradiso

An ibex with great, back-swept, scimitar-shaped horns perches on a crag's pinnacle with perfect equilibrium. Effortlessly, it leaps across a bare cliff face, appearing to stick to the sheer rock like a fly on a wall. This species of wild goat lives high above the tree line in the Alps and is responsible for the existence of two national parks. Together, the parks form one of the largest nature reserves in Western Europe.

A mountaineer climbing a knife-sharp ridge near Mont Blanc's 15,771-foot summit has one boot in France and the other in Italy. Looking south from Western Europe's highest mountain, the climber can trace the international boundary along a line of mountain crests. Two independent national parks meet along the border.

Both parks belong to the same geographical unit, the Graian Alps, but an imaginary political line designates one side the Italian Alps and the other the French Alps. Gran Paradiso National Park, Italy's oldest and most famous protected reserve, was established in 1922 with most of its 270 square miles lying above 5,000 feet. La Vanoise became France's first national park in 1963. The French government reserved 204 square miles of mountain wilderness to reinforce Gran Paradiso's mission to save the ibex.

By 1800, the ibex had been hunted almost to extinction in Europe. Its meat was excellent, its horns made magnificent trophies, but most keenly sought after was a small cross-shaped bone near its heart that was widely believed to possess magical powers. Fewer than a hundred ibex found final refuge around 13,323-foot Gran Paradiso, the highest mountain lying entirely inside Italy. King Victor Emmanuel II made the area a royal hunting preserve in 1856 to save the species. His grandson, Victor Emmanuel III, donated the lands to the Italian state, and Gran Paradiso National Park came into being between the northern cities of Aosta and Turin—one of the first national parks in Europe.

Today, Italy's high-speed *autostradas,* linked to France and Switzerland by mountain tunnels, allow vacationers easy access to Gran Paradiso's five valleys with their spectacular views and occasional glimpses of ibex. Villages rim the park with recreational facilities, hotels and restaurants, boosting Italy's important tourist industry.

Ibex increased in the park to more than 4,500 after World War II, but

Powerful male ibex prepare to clash horns in ritualized combat for dominance, their divided hooves ensuring firm footing on perilous crags. Saved from extinction at Gran Paradiso by Italy's former kings, ibex have returned to many Alpine areas in this century. National parks in Italy, France, Switzerland, and Austria protect them from hunters.

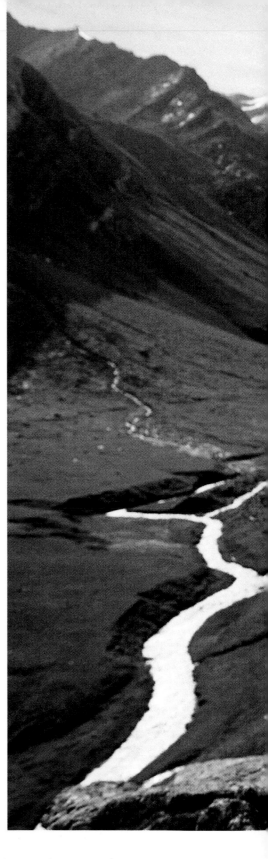

Twin lakes glisten deep in the Orco Valley of Gran Paradiso National Park. Wild, narrow valleys, like Orco, on the park's southern side attract nature lovers and hikers. Spectacular valleys to the north, accessible from major roads in the Aosta Valley, receive some commercial development as the Alps attract vacationers from all over the world. Gran Paradiso and its French twin, Vanoise National Park, maintain true wilderness at their cores but permit varying degrees of activity on the periphery.

as they multiplied they wandered into unprotected mountains where they once again became easy prey for hunters. French naturalists had pushed for a large ibex sanctuary like Gran Paradiso since the 1930s. Local people, however, resented any interference with their farming activities. A compromise was reached in 1963, when Vanoise National Park was set up with a wild, strictly controlled nature reserve at its center. A buffer zone nearly three times as large as the park allowed the normal population to gain its livelihood under less stringent regulations.

Vanoise and Gran Paradiso extended their common boundary in 1974. They share the same mixture of high-elevation habitats— forests of red fir, larch, and pine, clear lakes, alpine meadows brimming with wildflowers, and soaring peaks. Ibex and thousands of smaller, daintier chamois climb the heights of rock, scree, and glacier. Forest and meadow shelter ermine, badger, and the comical, whistling marmot. Many species of birds nest in the parks, some solitary like the circling golden eagle, others gregarious like the flocks of black Alpine chough, acrobatic cousins of the crow, that tumble and dart among the crags in close formation.

The wilderness of Vanoise remains strictly monitored by the French government, a domain for plants, wildlife, and climbers who hike among its well-managed mountain huts. It has served as a model for other, newer French national parks.

As tourism at Gran Paradiso continues to increase, nature lovers complain of damage to the trails and of trash strewn about the valleys, while prospering mountain villagers see this as a cost of the park's popularity. Park

administrators say that pressure from local vested interests to loosen the park's ecological regulations has eased somewhat as the area population recognizes the boost to their economy that comes from having a world-class wilderness in their backyard. In the meantime, the winner on both sides of the border is clearly the splendid ibex.

White as nearby glaciers, puffball mushrooms are among some 1,500 plant species—including rare Ice Age relicts—that thrive in Gran Paradiso's park.

Temperate Forest

When autumn frost nips the broad leaves of maple, ash, elm, and oak, trees announce the new season with a burst of color. Crimson, gold, and russet hues spread in an irregular band through temperate latitudes clear around the globe. From the Mississippi to the Atlantic, across the breadth of Europe, to China and Japan in east Asia, deciduous lowland forests begin to drop their leaves. A mild climate, short, cold winters, and adequate rainfall sustain this ever changing biome lying roughly between the tropics and the polar regions. In the Southern Hemisphere, smaller temperate forests of South America, Australia, and New Zealand are dominated by evergreen species which produce no autumn glow.

Cooler days affect countless woodland populations—opossums in Appalachia, wood warblers in France, Ryukyu rabbits in Japan—for the temperate forest shelters more fauna than any other midlatitude biome. Insects disappear in winter; many birds migrate to warmer climates; and a variety of furbearing animals curl up for a long nap.

The forest rests. When spring brings birdsong and a carpet of wildflowers, big animals such as deer, bear, and wild boar find ample food. A myriad of tiny creatures move through the warming earth. As tree buds open into summer leaves, birds nest in low shrubs and sunlit canopy. Squirrels, hedgehogs, and other woodland mammals raise their young in hidden places. Shade-loving plants take over the forest floor. At every level, plants and animals cooperate to keep their habitat in ecological balance.

Sometimes a single species of tree grows taller and dominates the others, as in New Jersey's beech forests or England's oak woods. On mountain slopes and in northerly latitudes, needle-leafed evergreens of the boreal forests mingle with deciduous trees. Two million years ago, such mixed forests covered much of the Northern Hemisphere.

As Ice Age glaciers advanced, animals and plants in North America retreated south along mountain valleys and returned when the ice melted. But in Europe whole forests perished, blocked by mountain chains that ran east to west from the Caucasus to the Pyrenees. When glaciers receded about 10,000 years ago, only 35 genera of European trees survived to reforest the continent.

Two-thirds of all temperate forests have now been cleared by growing human populations. Urban development and a desire for wood products speeded their disappearance. As forests diminished, people came to value this precious, renewable resource more. Laws now protect woodlands almost everywhere, and forests are carefully managed to benefit humans. But when they are replanted

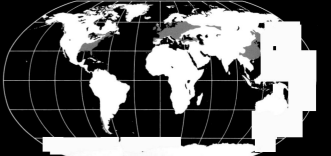

■ Temperate forest

primarily with trees that bring economic profit, forests lose their natural complexity and wildlife habitats vanish.

Despite conservation efforts, the biome continues to shrink. In industrialized countries, acid rain and other forms of pollution are the worst enemies. Fifty percent of Germany's forests are said to be dead or dying. In Asia, floods and erosion increase as deciduous forests are cut down for firewood, the only fuel for millions of people. But forests can renew themselves, and human intelligence could save them if it would.

In the heart of the Białowieża Forest in Poland (above), vast stands of oak and spruce, typical of the temperate forest biome, reach for the sky. Ancient trees and saplings tangled together create a perfect refuge for the forest's many inhabitants, including wolves, lynx, and the majestic European bison.

Białowieża

The deep forest lives in twilight beneath a dense, leafy canopy. The forest floor is a jumble of fallen trees slowly decaying under mantles of moss and fern and tangled undergrowth. Wildflowers brighten the occasional swampy clearings where sunshine penetrates. The heart of Poland's Białowieża Forest has remained in a state of natural neglect for thousands of years, its cycles of life and death scarcely touched by humans.

Remnant of the primeval forest that once covered much of lowland Europe, Białowieża is a mixture of broad-leafed trees and evergreens. Among its 26 species, mighty oaks may live for half a millennium and soar to 140 feet, while spruce and fir, a mere couple of centuries in age, tower even taller. Appropriately, Europe's largest wild mammals roam through the underbrush—moose, known in Europe as elk, along with red deer, lynx, and the European bison, or wisent, as imposing as its portrait on Ice Age cave walls. Large birds nest in the canopy—stork, eagle, and owl.

Białowieża's vast, 580 square miles of woodland spreads into two watersheds, whose rivers flow north to the Baltic and south to the Black Sea. On a political map, it straddles the border of Poland and Belarus, traditional line between Central and Eastern Europe. Poland claims about two-fifths of the forest, including the virgin wilderness at its core. Parts are managed by the government as a source of national income, but deep at its center, Białowieża National Park is a treasured laboratory for scientific study. In 1977, UNESCO recognized the park as a biosphere reserve and two years later named it a world heritage site. This area was enlarged in 1992.

While Europe's forests were relentlessly cleared for agriculture after the Middle Ages, sparsely populated Białowieża was rescued by its rich wildlife. From 1589, Polish kings kept the forest under royal protection as a game preserve where only royalty could hunt the rare bison, extinct in Western Europe. After Poland was partitioned in 1795, Russia's tsars appropriated Białowieża for their own hunting ground. Bison numbers had dwindled to about 700 by World War I.

In 1919 poachers killed the last wild bison in Białowieża. In that same year, national boundaries were redrawn throughout Europe and newly independent Poland received the wildwood area of Białowieża Forest. Poland quickly established a protected nature reserve of 17.5 square miles near its

Autumn frost spangles the branches of white birch as the sun rises over Białowieża Forest. The largest surviving remnant of Europe's primeval, mixed-tree forest sprawls across parts of Poland and neighboring Belarus. Polish scientists carry on extensive research at its ancient heart, Białowieża National Park, while strictly protecting it from human interference.

present border with Belarus, between the north-flowing Narewka River and its tributary, the Hwozna.

Białowieża National Park was formally opened in 1932, and intensive scientific studies of the area's flora and fauna began. The rare European beaver was found to have left the forest, but the extinct wild bison was replaced by breeding six captive wisent, some from zoos in Sweden and Germany. Their herd had grown to 16 when Nazi Germany invaded Poland in 1939. Ironically, Hermann Göring, Hitler's second-in-command, protected Białowieża's wildlife throughout the occupation, intending to make it his own private hunting reserve after the war.

The national park was restored in 1947, with a scientific council to advise its dedicated administrators. Permanent observation areas in the forest fostered much scientific research, making Białowieża National Park perhaps the most studied, cataloged, and protected wilderness in Europe. Botanists have identified some 40 different plant communities on the forest floor, including orchids and more than 3,000 varieties of fungus.

The Lesna River winds darkly through the southern end of the Białowieża Forest, breaking the monotony with occasional marshy meadows (below). For many centuries, Polish kings, Russian tsars, even Nazi general Hermann Göring, preserved the Białowieża Forest and its precious wildlife from destruction by proclaiming it their private hunting preserve. Rarest of all its creatures, the wisent, or European bison (opposite), has survived since the Ice Age, despite almost total extinction in the 1920s.

Białowieża

Ornithologists keep watch on 120 kinds of forest-nesting birds. Zoologists study thousands of insect species and some 50 mammals, noting the return of beavers and the new arrival of fox-like raccoon dogs from the Far East. More than 500 bison are carefully pedigreed and monitored.

But tolerance of human interference extends no farther than tracking lynx and marten by radio collars and feeding bison in winter to prevent them from stripping off the barks of trees. If lightning caused a forest fire, the park's administrators would doubtless let it burn itself out. In 1960 they resisted temptation to save a 600-year-old tree by surgery. On that day, the historic King Jagiello Oak was allowed to fall, and a press conference was called to bid it farewell.

Visitors are warmly welcomed to Białowieża National Park but they are closely supervised in the forest. Guides accompany them through a restricted area, then deliver them to the museum and educational facilities of a village that has grown up outside. Most visitors are Polish. School children come on regular field trips and receive intensive education in natural history and ecology. Groups of state factory workers appear frequently, but the park's remote location helps make foreign tourists a minority.

For all its care, Białowieża is not secure. Its ecosystem is threatened by air pollution, which has already inflicted massive damage in industrialized southern Poland. Rivers grow increasingly polluted, and habitats are threatened. Even the successful bison now suffer from overpopulation and inflict damage on trees because their natural enemy, the wolf, has almost disappeared. Surplus bison must be transferred to herds elsewhere or culled.

Buffer zones were added to the park after it was restored in 1947, but it remained too small for some animals. Moose, lynx, and wolf need very large territories, as do spotted eagles, cranes, and eagle owls. When wanderers strayed beyond the park's protection, they often perished. In the 1990s environmentalists began pressuring the Polish government to act, and, thanks to public demonstrations, they succeeded. The prime minister of Poland signed a decree almost doubling the park's protected area on July 16, 1996, and Białowieża was given a new lease on life.

Bison

When a poacher's bullet killed the last wild European bison (*Bison bonasus*) in Białowieża in 1919, extinction of the magnificent forest-dweller seemed certain. However, its close relative, the slightly smaller, shaggier buffalo of the American plains *(Bison bison)*, had returned from the brink of extinction around 1890 through careful breeding and protection. Following the United States' example, European scientists reestablished the European bison in Poland's primeval forest on a base of six zoo-bred animals. Several herds now exist in Europe. Initial fears that the tiny gene pool would result in problems of infertility or deformity have proved unfounded so far.

Białowieża

Evening ground fog shrouds a meadow in Białowieża's dense forest. Glades, bogs, and river washes allow sunlight to penetrate, nurturing a wide variety of flowering plants. In winter, park officials deposit hay in forest openings to discourage bison from stripping off tree bark.

A white stork (above), one of Europe's largest birds, stands silhouetted against the setting sun on its enormous tree-top nest. Other giants, such as cranes, owls, and eagles, also nest in Białowieża's spacious canopy.

Other Wild Places

Hohe Tauern

Austria The peaks of Hohe Tauern are unforgettably spectacular, situated near Austria's southern border, in the eastern Alps. Austria's largest protected landscape is part of a 70-mile-long mountain range composed of granite, gneiss, and schist with 12,457-foot Grossglockner, Austria's highest mountain, at its center. A high, winding road opened the formerly impenetrable region to visitors in 1935, and the drive offers panoramic views at almost every turn—perennial snowfields, glaciers, evergreen forests, waterfalls. A spur of the road gives a close-up look at the base of Grossglockner's massive, 5.9-mile-long Pasterze Glacier. Equally awesome is Austria's highest cataract, the Krimml Falls, tumbling 1,247 feet in the park's northwest corner. Hohe Tauern's wild center is rich in Alpine plants. Wildflowers and butterflies fill the high meadows with color in summer. Ibex, reintroduced from Gran Paradiso, and nimble chamois scale the rocky peaks. Golden eagles, vultures, and lammergeiers, a rare type of vulture, glide over forests and meadows, hunting for unwary small creatures such as marmots and hares. Hohe Tauern is a mecca for naturalists and all varieties of mountain lovers.

CHAMOIS IN HIGH TATRA NATIONAL PARK

Tatra and High Tatra National Parks

Poland/Slovakia The Tatras, highest range of the Carpathian Mountains, are rugged like the Alps, with steep, rocky sides, lakes, and forests. The peaks, all below 9,000 feet, are lacking in glaciers and perennial snow, yet the Tatras offer some of the most beautiful hiking and skiing in Eastern Europe. The border between Poland and Slovakia follows summits of this 40-mile range. The neighbors established a transborder protected area after World War II, an example followed by many other countries that shared wild places across their borders. Poland's Tatra National Park occupies about a third of the area, with relict forests of dwarf mountain pine, stone pine, and spruce. Slovakia's larger park, 280 square miles, is named High Tatra

MOUNTAIN LAKE, HIGH TATRA NATIONAL PARK

Last Wild Places

National Park to distinguish it from another park in the Low Tatras. Upland meadows and high cliffs make a habitat for chamois and marmots. Deer, wildcat, and rare brown bear roam the mixed forests, but like many other reserves, the Tatras are threatened by growing numbers of visitors and by airborne pollution from heavy industries.

Hardangervidda National Park

Norway Europe's highest mountain plateau is a vast, lonely wilderness in southern Norway. Hardangervidda National Park covers some 1,320 square miles of bleak, rocky, almost treeless peaks and valleys. The base elevation of 4,000 feet keeps its many lakes icebound for much of the year. Two climate zones give Hardangervidda a rich and varied plant life. The western rim, near the fjords, abounds in plants of northern Europe, while Arctic species and mosses thrive in the harsh eastern side. A moss discovered in Hardangervidda led to the development of cyclosporin, an important antirejection drug. About 50 kinds of birds from both temperate and Arctic zones come to breed in the undisturbed wilderness. Mammals are fewer, but among them is Europe's largest herd of wild reindeer, some 1,400 strong. which uses the entire park as its feeding and trekking ground. When snow disappears in summer, good trails and a number of overnight huts bring enthusiastic hikers and nature watchers to the wild, stark plateau.

Vikos Gorge

Greece A hidden gorge in Greece's remote Pindus Mountains is so wild and dramatic that people call it "Greece's Grand Canyon." Vikos Gorge lies in the rocky, sparsely populated region of Zagoria, near the Albanian border, where mountain folk keep many old customs alive. Vikos-Aoos National Park protects both remarkable natural sites and the scattered, tumble-down villages of two adjacent valleys. The eight-mile gorge, more than a thousand feet deep, is carved into limestone by the icy Voidomatis River. Dense pine and beech forests in precipitous side canyons conceal brown bears, wild boar, wolves, and lynx. Egyptian and griffon vultures, among the many birds that nest in the gorges, point up the wild, secluded nature of its depths. A deserted, partially

TREKKERS IN HOHE TAUERN NATIONAL PARK

restored medieval monastery looks down from a dizzying cliff top. Twin villages perched beneath jagged rock palisades at the mouth of Vikos Gorge welcome the experienced hikers who savor this difficult, unspoiled piece of wilderness.

Gennargentu Mountains

Italy Sardinia, Italy's untamed Mediterranean island, conjures up images of taciturn shepherds, feuding clans, and bandits. Times are changing, but the inhospitable Gennargentu massif on Sardinia's east coast remains one of Italy's most rugged wildernesses. Woodlands of pine and evergreen oak, and tough, drought-resistant scrub cover 390 square miles of wild upland. Gorges and ravines plunge to the sea from elevations over 5,000 feet. Snakes, scorpions, and spiders thrive here. The best-known inhabitants are some 150 mouflon, wild sheep with impressive curled horns that live in a reserve that keeps out domestic flocks grazing nearby. Rarer than mouflon are a handful of monk seals that survive in Sardinia's sheltered coves. A few lammergeiers, very rare large vultures, swoop over the dry scrubland, along with golden eagles, kites, and goshawks. A suggested reserve on the Bay of Orosei at the foot of the mountains would give protection to European leaf-toed geckos, Sardinian cave salamanders, loggerhead sea turtles, and other rare reptiles and amphibians. It is hoped that the entire Gennargentu area will be come a national park in the foreseeable future.

Astrakhan State Nature Reserve

Russia The Volga River delta's Astrakhan Nature Reserve is a large wetland bird sanctuary surrounded by dry plains and steppes at the north end of the Caspian Sea. Its mosaic of marshes teems with fish, frogs, and insects and supports huge colonies of cormorants, great egrets, herons, and a host of other birds. This wetland is vital to some 250 bird species that migrate every year from northern Europe and Asia including greylag geese, mute swans, and a variety of ducks. Wild boar frequent the marshes, too, along with 16 other mammals. In 1919, Lenin made the delta the first nature reserve of the newly founded Soviet Union. Though many more protected reserves followed, Astrakhan remained in special category, closely monitored and restricted to scientific study. Russia is now just one of five countries that share the Caspian Sea. They are still seeking agreement on common fishing and shipping regulations, while ecologists at the Astrakhan Nature Reserve worry about diminishing numbers of fish in the Caspian and future oil spills. The Volga Delta was designated a UNESCO Biosphere Reserve in 1984.

ARCTIC OCEAN

Ob
Yenisey
Lower Tunguska *u*
Lena
Lena
R U S S I A
Irtysh
Ob
Angara
Amur
Amur
Ussuri
USSURILAND
Lake
Baikal
Lake Baikal
Biosphere
Reserve

TURKEY
GEORGIA
AZERBAIJAN
CYPRUS
ARMENIA
KAZAKSTAN
Ertis
MONGOLIA
JAPAN
LEBANON
*Aral
Sea*
NORTH
KOREA
SYRIA
ISRAEL
IRAQ
TURKMENISTAN
UZBEKISTAN
KYRGYZSTAN
GOBI DESERT
JORDAN
T I A N   S H A N   *Turfan
Depression*
SOUTH
KOREA
KUWAIT
Pik
Pobedy
24,406 ft
7,439 m
C H I N A
SAUDI
ARABIA
IRAN
TAJIKISTAN
Pamirs
K U N L U N   M O U N T A I N S
Yellow
BAHRAIN
Karakoram
Range
Chang Tang
Reserve
Yangtze
Yangtze
QATAR
AFGHANISTAN
H
U.A.E.
PAKISTAN
I
Wolong
Natural
Reserve
Rub al-Khali
Indus
M
Brahmaputra
YEMEN
OMAN
Ganges
NEPAL
A
BHUTAN
Sagarmatha N.P.
L
*Arabian
Sea*
BANGLADESH
A
MYANMAR
INDIA
Y
PHILIPPINES
Sundarbans
A
LAOS
THAILAND
Mekong
VIETNAM
I N D I A N
CAMBODIA
Sepilok
Reserve
SRI
LANKA
Kinabalu Park
O C E A N
Gunung Mulu N.P.
BRUNEI
M A L A Y S I A
Danum
Valley
Conservation
Area
SINGAPORE
Borneo

I N D O N E

Java

0   600 Mi
0   1000 Km

Asia

by Patrick R. Booz

Deserts and rain forests, islands and steppes, mountains and marshlands, Asia's breathtaking geographic variety covers nearly one-third of the world's landmass. It claims the highest and lowest points on earth— Mount Everest and the Dead Sea. Arabian sands contrast with Russia's tundra wastes. An unbroken grassland rolls for more than a thousand miles from the borders of Europe to Mongolia. At the continent's heart converges the world's greatest cluster of high ranges, the Himalaya, Karakoram, Hindu Kush, Pamirs, and Kunlun. Tropical lands to the south hold jungles of dreamlike birds. China boasts the finest flora in the world, with perhaps 30,000 known species.

Asia's claim to genuinely wild places is sound. Parts of the Brahmaputra River Gorge of eastern Tibet have never seen humans. Much of Siberia's taiga, the world's largest forest, remains inviolate. But glance at a population map and the Asian wilderness becomes suddenly diminished. The great river valleys—Indus, Ganges, Mekong, Pearl, Yangtze, Yellow—teem with people. Three of every five humans are Asian. The island of Java alone has more than 100 million people. China's Sichuan province has just under 110 million.

Hunger for housing, agricultural land, fuelwood, minerals, and animal products makes the challenge for preserving biological diversity especially great in Asia, where destruction of magnificent ecosystems is most advanced. Yet this situation shows some hope. Environmentalists in China and members of the world conservation community recently rallied to the cause of the golden monkey, threatened by logging, and in Malaysia, education programs about conservation have entered schools. Small, local contributions that help both people and nature offer the best way to proceed.

Crowning glory of a tropical dawn, Mount Kinabalu rises to 13,455 feet, high above the rain forests of Sabah, east Malaysia. This granite upthrust ascends in a series of astonishing ecological zones that contain half the world's families of flowering plants, including 1,200 types of orchids.

Borneo

A hot, humid dusk tensely awaits the first flittings, then the muffled roar. The great cave mouth disgorges a seemingly endless stream of bats, many thousands of them, in an awesome display. Here, at Sarawak's Gunung Mulu National Park, the winged mammals head out for a night of eating in an ancient rain forest that contains astounding caves.

Borneo, the world's third largest island, straddles the Equator and forms a patchwork of three nations, Indonesia, tiny Brunei, and Sabah and Sarawak states of east Malaysia.

Millions of years ago, Borneo became squeezed between the Australian and Asian tectonic plates, buckling the Mulu region and exposing its limestone formations to acidic rain. Eons ate at them steadily. First discovery of the cave system by outsiders goes back to 1961. A Royal Geographical Society expedition in 1977-78 brought in 130 scientists; then speleologists made the big finds in 1980.

Deer Cave's yawning entrance, largest cave mouth in the world, runs for more than a mile. Cascading from above are 600-foot waterfalls. Clearwater Cave works its way back to a clear, rushing river, then plunges on for an incredible 32 miles, perhaps the world's longest cavern. To finish the superlatives, Sarawak Chamber expands upwards as earth's largest rock chamber, able to hold several football fields.

Outside in dappled light grows a unique, single-leaved palm, representative of Mulu's 1,500 flowering plants. Mount Mulu itself rises to 7,795 feet, and beyond are the Pinnacles, outlandish 150-foot limestone daggers that shoot up above the trees.

Within the caves waits a nightmarish world of weirdly adapted animals. Thumb-size bats and their larger brethren, flying foxes, create a carpet of noxious, slimy feces, inhabited by glowing guano worms, fed upon by coprophagous cockroaches. Blind snakes grope in search of blind spiders and crickets with hugely extended antennae. Transparent crabs crawl away. In this subterranean world live flocks of swiftlets, the only birds with sonar to let them fly in complete darkness. More than 260 species of birds reside in Mulu, among them the regal rhinoceros hornbill, emblem of Sarawak, perched high in the tropical canopy. It shouts forth an unforgettable series of roars, which, once heard, resound forever as part of the jungle's soul.

A playful orang-utan (opposite) swings by at Borneo's Sepilok Reserve. Asia's only great ape, the orangutan lives solely in jungles of Sumatra and Borneo. Mouth agape, a crested lizard pauses in dense under-growth, while a goggle-eyed tarsier clutches a tree with specially adapted fingers that provide suction.

Arab traders and Ming-dynasty porcelain merchants from China came to north Borneo, but the important story involves the Penan people, members of Malaysia's last surviving nomadic tribe. After caring for their own needs, they traded rare animal parts and organs to the Chinese, who valued the Bornean products as powerful medicines.

Most Penan have now settled down as farmers. Some Penan have adopted guns, but a few still shape blowguns from the *belian* ironwood tree and bring down game with poison darts. These last hunters are the final repository of ancient forest lore.

North of Mulu in Sabah state reigns 13,455-foot Mount Kinabalu, a masterpeice of nature at the heart of Kinabalu National Park, where half the world's families of angiosperms—the flowering plants—are represented through ascending vegetative zones. Lowland dipterocarps, the outstandingly tall and precious hardwood trees, give way around 4,000 feet to a mixed montane forest of tropical oaks, proud chestnuts, magnolias, nutmegs, and cinnamon. Off the trail, at the edge of a swollen waterfall in a misty downpour, the Borneo rain forest becomes a total environment of wetness and greenness, of pungent fragrances and sensual delight.

Soon comes the the richest of all, the cloud forest, the zone of bamboos, ferns and mosses, between 6,500 and 8,000 feet. Most of Kinabalu's

Rain forest river meanders through the Danum Valley Conservation Area (opposite) in eastern Sabah's Brassey Range. Wonderfully rich in plant and animal species, this hilly zone supports Asia's largest remnant population of wild elephants. Such hardwood forests nurture

Borneo's rafflesia, world's largest flower—three feet in diameter—a bizarre parasitic plant with five fleshy petals that stink and begin to rot soon after they emerge. Pollination comes from a carrion fly, attracted by the foul decaying odor.

1,200 orchid types are here. Graceful pitcher plants, some up to a foot long, can hold enough water to nourish a special, miniature pool of life. They can also drown a mouse. Cloud, light and shadow play amidst the foliage as temperatures drop. At last arrives the summit realm of mere sedges and grass, but views to the South China Sea and across the breadth of North Borneo compensate for any lack of plants. In the forests below creep 150,000 insect species, 200 reptiles and amphibians, nine kinds of technicolor tree frogs and mouse deer only a foot high at the shoulder, an easy mouthful for a python. Far below, too, are the park's 80 fig species, vital food source for fruit bats and many other animals. The celebrated rafflesia, the plant kingdom's largest flower at three feet in diameter, crops up strangely through a complex, parasitic existence. It has no leaves or roots, but flowers with five thick petals, then promptly begins to stink and rot, attracting carrion flies for pollination.

Kinabalu possesses an undulating plain of raw granite at the top. Morning rain throws sheets of water off the peak. On the mountain's east flank an unexplored, mile-deep chasm called Low's Gully became a source of drama in March 1994. Ten British commandos descended on an adventure exercise. Death nearly took them, rescue coming only after four weeks. The mountain's reputation for wildness remained.

Kadazan people inhabit the Kinabalu region. Their language provided the name: *aki nabalu*, "revered place of the dead". This is their sacred mountain, and they want it to last forever.

The creation of national parks at Mulu and Kinabalu brings formal protection to trees and habitats, but also opens the door to steadily increasing hordes of tourists. The price of protection is controlled development and a slow erosion of the last wild places.

Logging at Mulu

Quick rewards come to illegal loggers who, with international connections, encroach on east Malaysia's rain forests. The view from river approaches to Gunung Mulu National Park reveals banks bereft of majestic hardwood trees. Now interior forests are falling, too. After logging, once wild jungles become more susceptible to fire. Environmental degradation follows and species fail. Local Penan tribesmen, Malaysia's last nomads, depend on nature's bounty in and around the park. As it goes, so goes their livelihood. The Penan have protested, the government promises to act, but corruption and timber company wealth make detection and prevention of illegal logging difficult.

Rub al-Khali

Like waves frozen in time on a vast, pale sea, dunes flow silently to every horizon. The Arabian Peninsula's southern third holds earth's largest unbroken expanse of sand, a quarter of a million square miles of brutally harsh desert. Such tracts of pure sand are rare, this one created in ancient times when volcanic highlands in the west and south and dry seabeds to the east lay exposed to the erosive powers of water and wind. These forces wore down the surfaces to create pebbles and grains; prevailing winds over the eons then swept up tiny particles to build gigantic mountains of sand approaching a thousand feet high.

Bedouins have called these wastes the Rub al-Khali, the Empty Quarter, or simply al-Ramlah, "the sands." Supremely hardy tribal people, their intimate knowledge of the desert has kept them alive while searching with their camels for sparse grazing grounds in a land where the norms are extreme heat—temperatures over 120°F—dehydration, withering winds, and chilly winter nights.

Sometimes years pass with no rain. Yet in this seemingly uninhabitable realm, salt bushes, a drought-adapted sedge, and virtually leafless abal bushes survive, and the sands may be brightened by the rich yellow flowers of the desert tribulus. Bedouins describe how a good steady rain of one day and one night is enough to keep the plants alive and the desert green for three or even four years, a crucial event in their traditional life.

Animals, too, survive in the Empty Quarter through conservation of moisture, perspiring less, urinating less, exhaling less vapor. The desert hare survives the summer by keeping to deep burrows by day. Another common mammal, the sand fox, feeds on rodents and reptiles, and requires no water. Seed birds thrive when plants go dry and seeds dehisce; insectivores become active when rain brings out the bugs. Birds live on the juices of insects; sand cats and other predators gain water from lizards and gerbils. Bedouins' greatest respect goes to the prince of the desert, the white oryx—*jawasi,* "he who does not drink." Sometimes it is called "doctor of the Arabs" for the belief in its curative powers. In shimmering heat the oryx appears white, with dark markings along its sides and face. Rising from its head are magnificent straight horns, more than two feet long.

Stark dunes create dreamlike patterns near Fasad, Oman. Named Rub al-Khali—the Empty Quarter—by nomads millennia ago, the immense sand desert of southern Arabia has ever been a harsh, little-visited place, where temperatures often rise above 120˚F.

Foreign travelers, mostly Englishmen, had long known of the Empty Quarter, but none had successfully crossed it. Not until 1931 did Bertram Thomas succeed, immediately followed by Harry St. John Philby, thus solving a great geographic conundrum. Although the Arabian American Oil Company (Aramco) had conducted a major expedition to the quarter's heart by 1938, as late as 1946 Bertram and Philby were the only two Europeans to have traversed the sands.

Rub al-Khali

In the late 1940s Aramco was building airstrips in the desert, and, mapping the blank spots with Bedouin guides, searching everywhere for oil. By the early 1960s the Empty Quarter map was complete. Widespread hunting from automobiles, even from aircraft, soon decimated the oryx and nearly finished off the desert bustard. A few small herds of oryx have been reintroduced to Oman to live again in the great inhospitable wilds.

Mysterious, burqa-clad Bedouin of Saudi Arabia (opposite) peers over colorful tent siding. Today, few brave the fiery sands in traditional ways—motor vehicles have largely replaced camels—though love of desert freedom persists. Sand dunes aligned in parallel rows appear to extend forever.

 Mountains

Among the most physically and emotionally spectacular environments on earth, mountain strongholds present us with a kaleidoscopic array of visual images—icebound, snow-covered peaks, precipitous cliffs, knife-blade ridges, pristine lakes in glaciated bowls, shadowy chasms, canyons, and gorges. In addition, their profiles create a wealth of distinct mountain ecological layers—from cold, bare-rock summits through alpine meadows and high tundra, coniferous woodlands and forests, rich deciduous foothill zones and finally, luxuriant valleys or open savannas.

Climbing through such layers, where temperatures drop 2°F for every 600 feet in elevation, can resemble a journey from equatorial tropics to Arctic barrens within a few vertical miles. Yet, almost like islands, each mountain—and in some instances each side of each mountain—possesses a unique ecology of plant and animal species that often bears little or no relationship to the broader regional environment. Collectively, they are key elements in the snowy-region "cryosphere," reflecting heat back into space by the albedo effect and helping to regulate global temperatures. Their sturdy appearance—seemingly the very epitome of timeless endurance—disguises a delicate fragility. At high elevations, slow-growth ecosystems are vulnerable to climatic or biological shock, and their steep slopes are ripe for erosion if protective vegetation layers are destroyed.

Sadly, despite the illusion of safe and pristine mountain frontiers, there are few remote or rugged enough to have escaped the threats of man. While up to 40 percent of the earth's surface can be classified as mountainous, our incessant demands upon these storehouses of natural resources for water, energy, minerals, timber, fuel, land development, and tourism are taking their toll. In such glorious regions as the Swiss Alps, a combination of acid rain eradication of snow-holding forests and the enormous demands of several million skiers annually have contributed to the rapid decline of plant and animal species throughout this region. Preservation efforts by such grassroots-coordinating groups as Alp Action are being closely watched by those hoping to save these wonderous examples of earth's wild places.

Mountains

Roiling clouds part
to reveal the
summit of Ultar
Peak in the
Karakoram Range.
This 24,238-foot

cathedral of
rock and ice,
surrounded by
glaciers and
craggy spires,
stands in Hunza,

northern Pakistan,
near the densest
concentration of
high mountains in
the world.

Stars wheel through the night sky around Mount Everest, monarch of the Himalaya at 29,028 feet. Earth's highest point honors George Everest, British surveyor general of India. Nepali call the mighty peak Sagarmatha, and Tibetans call it Chomolungma, both names meaning "mother of the universe".

Sagarmatha

Howling winter winds strip the mountain's snows to reveal immense black granite walls, sending eastward a telltale streamer of white from the summit, highest point of the world's highest national park. Mount Everest, known to Nepali as Sagarmatha, "mother of the universe," stands as the centerpiece of Sagarmatha National Park, a 480-square-mile wonderland located in northeast Nepal along the border with Tibet.

Tremendous earth forces threw up the Himalayan giants only several million years ago, making them among the world's youngest mountains. Sharp peaks, razor ridges, stark faces, and avalanches reveal the living power of rain, wind, ice, and glaciers to shape the terrain. The Khumbu Icefall's jumbled magnificence, just above Everest Base Camp, is the first obstacle for mountaineers but a glaciologist's dream.

This unsurpassed vertical realm descends nearly 20,000 feet from the crest of the Himalaya through three distinct vegetation zones. Just below permanent snow are lichens, mosses, dwarf grasses, and the weird *Saussurea gossypiphora,* a ground-hugging, fibrous plant that creates a tiny microclimate to protect itself from the cold. Slowly, the descent reveals bursts of color: bright primulas, gentians, Himalayan edelweiss, glittering yellow alpine cinquefoil. Here is the alpine scrub zone, between 13,000 and 16,500 feet, where once every few years the reds, pinks, and whites of *Rhododendron arboreum* emerge simultaneously to turn rugged brown hills a gentle raspberry. Beneath the alpine scrub lie true forests, though these are not extensive in the park.

Blue Himalayan pine, elegant with five-needle foliage and drooping cones, and silver fir, with handsome, upright cones, are the dominant conifers. Birch and juniper also grow here, the latter reaching nearly 50 feet in height near temples, where they are protected.

Water, sustenance of life, comes from two sources: constant melt and runoff from the mountains and heavy monsoon downpours that arrive unfailingly each June. Three-fourths of Sagarmatha's annual 40 inches of rain fall in the summer to create a short, dripping, fecund season.

The park's boundaries embrace some 28 mammal species, including two species of bats and many rodents. Larger animals, high up, have

Silhouetted against Nuptse's vertical wall, a solitary trekker inside Sagarmatha National Park crosses a glacier to seek views of Mount Everest. Silence and nature's grandeur draw thousands of visitors each year. Below, a lone tahr stands on a precipice. This short-horned goat-antelope inhabits the steepest parts of the park near the tree line, but descends to lower elevations in spring to eat succulent new growth.

adapted to thin air and freezing temperatures, the noble snow leopard with a thick coat and great stealth, the black bear with fur and large lungs. Himalayan tahr are agile, powerful wild-goatlike animals, the male unmistakable with yellow mane and curling horns. The ingenious marmot has survived as the world's highest living mammal by staying compact with short limbs to reduce body heat loss. The nocturnal lesser panda, a russet bundle of fur with masked face and thick, striped tail, lives in the lower forest zone, happily eating bamboo, with a sixth finger for grasping the stems. Sagarmatha's 118 bird species include the dazzling Impeyan pheasant, national bird of Nepal, known as the *danphe,* "nine-colors." Choughs, clowns and acrobats of the heights, have been spotted twisting and diving at 27,000 feet. Blood pheasants, flaming red at eye, beak, claw, and tail, scurry in the birch forests, and the golden eagle glides above as the park's primary raptor. A curious creature is the brown dipper, an aquatic bird with a huge oil gland that protects its feathers from freezing water and specialized lids that cover its nostrils.

For all its variety and grandeur, Sagarmatha National Park is a fragile place. None know this better than the Sherpas who migrated here from Eastern Tibet 400 years ago. Surviving as pastoralists and traders, they called the area Khumbu. Their Buddhist heritage identified this gem of nature as a *beyul,* or sacred sanctuary, that would stand as a refuge when the world faced dire calamities. The Sherpas have always lived in harmony with the land, though their home of between 2,500 and 3,500 people is under severe pressure from tourism.

Among the first foreigners to gaze into Khumbu was the British mountaineer George Mallory in 1921, from high on the Tibetan side of Mount Everest. Another mountaineer, New Zealander Edmund Hillary, conquered Everest with the Sherpa Tenzing Norgay in 1953. Out of that remarkable feat grew Hillary's deep concern for the region and his profound respect for the strength and personal qualities of the Sherpas. His efforts led to the creation of the park in 1976 and its inclusion as a UNESCO world heritage site in 1979.

Sagarmatha

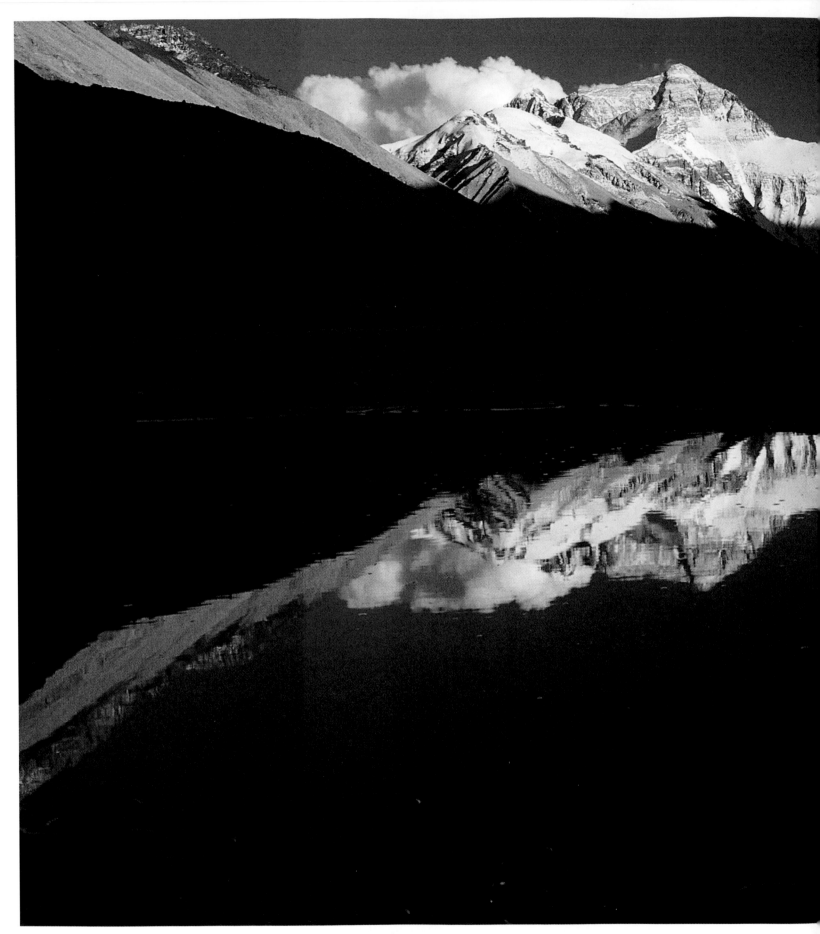

A pool of glacial meltwater mirrors the pristine image of Mount Everest below Tibet's Rongbuk Glacier. No mountain has received more attention: Height, remoteness, drama, and romance have motivated more than 500 people to reach its summit since the first ascent in 1953.

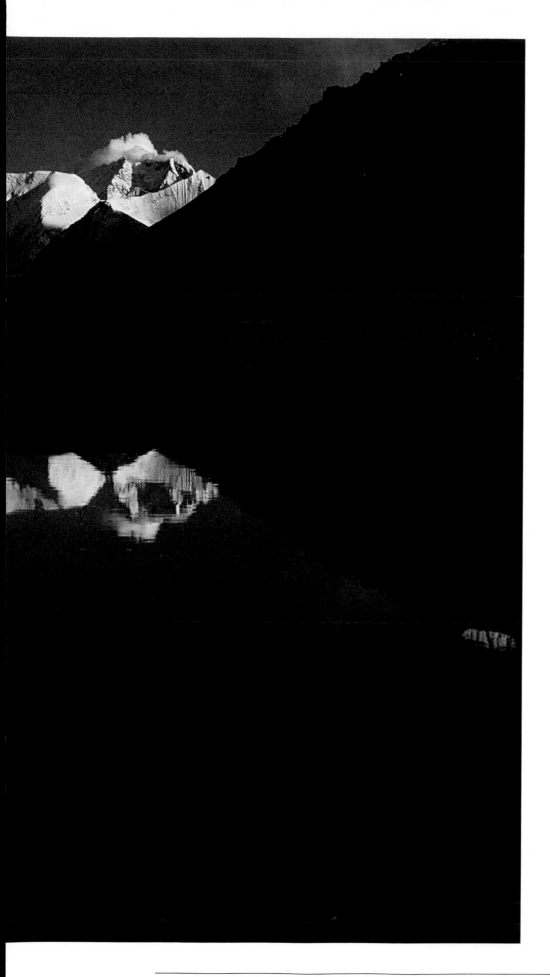

Impact of Tourism

In 1953 two men stood alone at the top of the world. Today, climbers have sometimes been forced to wait their turn making the ascent to the great peak's summit. A yearly flood of some ten thousand tourists and trekkers places great demands on Sagarmatha. Local Sherpas benefit, but the results are deforestation, over-grazing, garbage *(below),* and a breakdown of traditional life. Hope lies in reforestation, technology—solar heaters, micro-hydropower stations— and education programs. Already strict rules prohibit sale of firewood to tourists, while rubbish pits and recy-cling projects help control solid waste. Revival of the indigenous village *shinga nawa*—forest guardianship committee—is an optimistic sign.

Boreal Forest

January stillness enshrouds a gloomy green expanse of identical trees. The world's largest uninterrupted woodland, boreal forests rim the top of the Northern Hemisphere, spanning Asia and Europe, hopping the Atlantic and continuing across North America, where they cover 40 percent of Canada. This high-latitude band, up to 1,500 miles wide, touches tundra in the north; to the south it gives way to grassland steppes and broadleaf temperate forests.

Eurasia's boreal woodland, known as taiga, stretches for 4,000 miles. Its makeup is simple, with usually one or two species, up to 75 feet tall, spreading over thousands of square miles. The trees are needle-leaf conifers—spruce, fir, larch, pine— all shaped, Christmas-tree-like, to shed snow. Slender trunks evade the worst winter gales (the name "boreal" comes from the Greek god Boreas, god of the north wind) and shallow roots soak up water.

Youthful boreal forests have colonized the vast north only over the past 10,000 years, after the retreat of the last Pleistocene ice. In Alaska, new spruce timberland grows where glaciers ruled just 200 years ago.

Summer's short growing season of almost continuous sun releases life's pent-up miracle. An eruption of color and activity comes over the boreal biome. Shoots sprout quickly as bogs display tiny flowers, iridescent dragonflies, brilliant butterflies and the green flash of frogs. Few animals live solely in the boreal biome. Shortage of food forces them southward to where temperate and coniferous forests merge. The brown bear, an eight- to ten-foot behemoth weighing in at up to 1,500 pounds, ranges over great tracts, omnivorously searching for berries, nuts, fungi, carrion, insects, fish, even deer to feed its bulk. Other beasts are the fearless wolverine and elk, North America's long-legged moose. Wolves, largely exterminated in the New World, thrive in Siberia with several subspecies. But all is not well.

Forests of softwood conifers, steadily sacrificed to satisfy worldwide hunger for houses, furniture and newsprint, are also cleared for farmland. Acid rain corrodes foliage; oil and mineral extraction damages the land and requires long pipelines. Sensible solutions to these problems exist, however: conifer plantations for raw materials, control of fossil fuel exploitation, creation of parks and refuges.

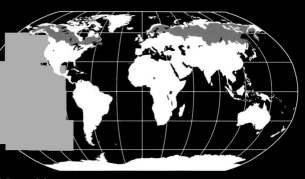

■ **Boreal forest**

Lake Baikal shore greets the realm of coniferous trees, a continuous forest stretching for 4,000 miles across Eurasia from the Baltic to the Pacific. Called taiga in Russian, the boreal biome circles the world's northen latitudes, with eight-month winters and bright, short summers of almost uninterrupted sunlight.

Winter ice traps a rocky promontory off Olkhon Island, midway point along Lake Baikal's 395-mile-long arc. Beneath the frozen surface lies one-fifth of the world's fresh water in a mile-deep trench created by tectonic forces 25 million years ago.

Lake Baikal

Emerging from the veil of green forests, through alleyways of trees parted by tumbling rivers, suddenly ahead spreads an azure vision.

Crisp golden light illuminates mighty Baikal, a lake of superlatives to match the hugeness of its Siberian homeland. Bending in a graceful 395-mile arc just north of Mongolia, it is the world's oldest lake and also the deepest, bottoming out at 5,371 feet. This ancient hollow holds 20 percent of the world's fresh water, its surface area the size of Belgium.

Remnants of extinct volcanoes dot Baikal's borders, reminders of seismic activity that shakes north Asia periodically. A terrible earthquake struck in 1861, inundating large areas and creating a new bay. Today, the lake is fed by runoff from surrounding mountains, some rising more than a mile above the lake. More than 300 rivers and streams flow in, but only one major river, the Angara, flows out, leading Baikal's waters to the Arctic Ocean. In August and September, sudden summer storms and tempestuous winds can wreak havoc. The worst is the wicked *sarma,* which can throw up 15-foot waves. Such displays of virility have ever been a curse to boatmen.

Baikal is large enough to have various microclimates—dry Olkhon Island, fit only for grasses, contrasts with saturated, lush eastern shore forests—and overall the weather is warmer than surrounding Siberia's. Still, freezes come hard in January—winter ice is more than three feet thick—and the thaw must wait until May. A brief warm summer draws vacationers from nearby Irkutsk, revelers who come to marvel at the water's cleanness and clarity, with visibility more than a hundred feet. Stout swimmers dive down openmouthed, swallowing great gulps of the cold, immaculate water.

But beyond simple summertime pleasures the spirit of Baikal goes much deeper into the hearts and souls of Russians. Called "sacred sea," it has been revered since time immemorial by the Evenks, largest and most widespread of Siberian tribes. Hunters, reindeer breeders, and pastoralists, they looked to their shamans to honor the lake with chants and prophecies. European Russians came to know and love it largely after the success of the Trans-Siberian Railway, which reached the lake's southern edge in 1899. Buddhist Buryat Mongols worship the gods of water, mountain, and forests.

Dense as fur, Siberia's renowned birches cover a mountainside near Lake Baikal's southern reaches. Birches take hold as glaciers recede or after conifer forests fall to ax or fire. An Old World horse-drawn sledge (left) slips across Baikal ice at dusk, keeping alive links with the past.

Attuned to the lake's ways, they are full of admiration and healthy fear of Baikal's power. Buryats mark peninsulas and holy islands here with offerings and amulets.

Siberian taiga of larch, birch, and pine dominates the shoreline. Hot springs amid the sea of trees nurture plant species that otherwise would have disappeared long ago or fled south to escape the last ice age. Baikal's very long life, dating from the late Oligocene epoch, when temperate, even subtropical conditions prevailed, has made the lake an evolutionary wonder.

The lake's most famous resident is the nerpa, or Baikal freshwater seal, most closely related to the arctic ringed seal 2,000 miles away.

Adaptation to freshening water allowed it to survive, though how exactly it made the transition from sea to isolated lake remains a mystery. Nerpa prefer islands, partly to evade their enemies, wolf and bear, though the seals can be found anywhere. They live mostly on *golomyanka*, a bizarre endemic fish that spends time thousands of feet below the surface. It has delicate fins and

Lake Baikal

nearly transparent skin that encases pounds of fatty flesh, a rich diet for the seals. Each spring, the 60,000 nerpa face a controlled slaughter that allows hunters to cull 6,000 of their number.

Baikal's complex ecology has a main hero, the humble crustacean *Epischura baicalensis,* a tiny creature near the bottom of the food chain but one that helps all others. It makes up 98 percent of the water's zooplankton, providing sustenance to so many other life-forms. It is also a champion of cleanliness, each organism acting as a minute filter; combined they remove vast amounts of algae and bacteria from the lake, creating a level of purity known in few places. Other natural filters are sponges and an incredible 250 varieties of shrimp.

Within the lake a rich and varied flora has taken hold—more than 600 plant species thrive on or near the surface. Twelve hundred animal species—including 52 different fish—swim, paddle, and float. Life at every level is allowed by sinking, oxygen-rich cold water that circulates throughout the deep lake. Warmer lakes lack this life-giving cycle because oxygen-bearing water always stays only near the surface. Above all these limnological miracles soar more than 320 types of birds.

A number of national parks and nature reserves, the first established in 1916, others only in 1987, act to protect the lake, the shoreline, and the surrounding mountains. The overarching Lake Baikal Region Biosphere Reserve now contains more endemics than any other reserve in the world—1,500 unique animal and plant species.

Siberian remoteness is no guarantee of Baikal's safety. Alarming threats—paper and pulp mills, mining, petrochemical stations, coal-fired power plants, a new railroad—all contribute to pollution. Worst of all is Baikalsk Cellulose-Paper Plant, producer of raw material for clothing. A blot on the nation, it damages both air and water. The lake's southern end already has seen the death of its bottom, and fish die-offs warn of broader degradation.

Luckily, Lake Baikal has its defenders—concerned scientists, conservationists, common folk—and from them shines the light of hope and survival.

Tectonics

Lake Baikal's great age and depth—creators of its unique biology—are due to tectonics, the forces that shape the earth's crust. The Baikal rift of the huge Eurasian plate formed the lake bed more than 25 million years ago, making the lake the earth's oldest. The rift continues to deepen, and Baikal widens by up to an inch a year. The exceptionally clean, mile-deep water plunges down to hydrothermal vents at several spots. Heat from beneath the lake emerges to foster strange life-forms around these vents—freshwater sponges and translucent shrimp and snails.

Gnarled, noble pine stands sentinel over Baikal's Peschanaya Bay (left). The peace belies a reality, however—air and water pollution threaten sections of Siberia's sacred sea. A nerpa, the

Baikal freshwater seal, (above) rests on a rock. Clumsy on land, the seal races gracefully under water to secure its diet of golomyanka, a fatty fish.

Under an auspicious rainbow, yaks head home at day's end, herded by a lone nomad. Across the Chang Tang, Tibet's wild northern plateau, extremes of temperature, dryness, and high elevation limit the number of humans.

Chang Tang

Powerful and free, wild yaks graze and canter in a remote enclave of wildest Tibet. Close relatives of the American bison, with heavy shoulders and shaggy hair streaming in the wind, they move gracefully on dainty hooves despite their bulk—a grown male can weigh 2,000 pounds. Forceful 30-inch horns lead the way in the search for new pastures. These proud sovereigns of the plateau have retreated to the Aru basin region, where the last few herds of wild yaks remain.

This basin lies within the western section of the Chang Tang Reserve, created by China in 1993 as the world's second largest conservation area, 600 miles wide and 300 miles long. Preservation of an entire huge ecosystem, one of the last true virgin expanses on the planet, is a daunting task but especially necessary for migrating animals always on the move.

Tibet has three main ecological zones: the relatively moist river gorge area in the southeast; an inner plateau with good grazing land, cultivation, and towns; and the forbidding outer plateau, where never ending landscapes of umber, grey, yellow, and soft reds suffer under a severe climate. The towering Himalayan range acts as a rain shadow, forcing summer monsoon wetness to drop on its southern faces. These green slopes rise in sharp contrast to the north, where the great plateau spreads away as a high altitude desert with only 5 to 10 inches of precipitation a year. Despite the rain shadow, fierce storms of sleet and snow can sweep down at any moment.

Tibetans call it *chang tang,* northern plain. "Raised" uplands of rolling hills, plains, and snowy mountains all lie between 15,000 and 17,000 feet, treeless and desolate, with constant winds and winter temperatures of minus 40°F. The reserve's southern part is its essential lifeline, with sufficient pasturage on grassy steppes amid dry lake basins and brackish lakes. Far from Tibet's main population centers, the Chang Tang has been home through the centuries to only small numbers of detemined nomads with their flocks of sheep, goats, and domesticated yaks.

Life appears sparse here in the wilderness, its dryness and altitude perennial challenges that limit growth, yet the Chang Tang is a realm that supports varied and admirable fauna. The Tibetan wild ass, or kiang, races across plateau flats at speeds up to 40 miles an hour. A herd on the horizon is a swift gray cloud in motion.

Tibetan antelopes forage for their lives amid frozen snow-covered plains. Only males sport the saberlike horns, used to ward off rivals during the early winter mating season. In summer, females and young move southward from distant birthing grounds, the last great migrations on the awe-inspiring plateau.

121

Summer migration of the Tibetan antelope is the Chang Tang's major spectacle. Thousands of females and young—unaccompanied by the larger males—move south from unknown birthing sites in the Kunlun Mountains and stream across the heights. A hundred years ago they would come in the tens of thousands, delicate and perfect in their environment. Now the timid antelopes are down to four migrating groups. Safe for the moment, the animals face threats in the form of hunters and trappers who pursue them for their beautiful soft wool, highly prized by the weavers of Kashmir.

Other precious animals are the blue sheep, snow leopard, wolf, lynx, Tibetan brown bear, and argali, a large Asiatic wild sheep with thick, curved horns. The endemic Tibetan woolly hare has long furry ears and elegant eyes. Its active, playful relative the pika sits up and chatters constantly, either to warn of danger or to stay in touch with other pikas. They form a vital part of the food chain—bears, wolves, cats, hawks, and falcons all feed on them. Birds over the Chang Tang number some 67 breeding species, with 6 endemic types.

The first Westerners to witness Tibet's bleak northern plateau were an odd mix of British military men, French aristocrats, American scholars, and quixotic travelers seeking a back door into the holy city of Lhasa. A fiery, indomitable Swede named Sven Hedin made three expeditions, the last in 1906-08, which produced intricate records, maps, and scientific publications on the Chang Tang. All who traveled there have been deeply moved by the land's strange, stark beauty.

Nomads historically hunt for subsistence, but the moment roads push into the interior no creature is safe. Vehicles can reach anywhere, and officials are known to abuse their positions by sponsoring junkets of illegal hunting. Remoteness and climatic hostility are at present the best protection for the Chang Tang Reserve, but man, too, must have a change of heart to safeguard this unparalleled gem of nature.

Shaggy Bactrian camels plod through remote valleys of Tibet's Chang Tang, leading scientists into one of earth's last virgin territories. Plateau residents include a Tibetan woolly hare, unique to the region, and two kiang, wild asses capable of streaking to the horizon at 40 miles an hour.

Other Wild Places

Pamir Mountains

Tajikistan, China Wild, windswept mountains in a tangled knot of Central Asian ranges, the Pamir (Marco Polo's original "Roof of the World") form much of the new nation of Tajikistan. Bounded by Afghanistan in the south, Kyrgyzstan in the north, and Chinese Turkistan's deserts in the east, Pamir peaks are mostly rounded domes spread amid high, frozen valleys, though to the west abrupt faces rise from dramatic canyonlands.

Glaciers abound, including 48-mile-long Fedchenko Glacier, one of the world's longest. The Pamir's two tallest peaks stand in China—25,325-foot Kongur and 24,757-foot Muztagata Ata, "father of ice mountains," a great whale-back that seems to rise gently forever. These two form an anchor to the eastern range, where desert-like conditions reign under glaring sunlight during an average of more than 300 clear days a year.

Rugged Tajik and Kyrgyz tribesmen move with their flocks of sheep and goats in summer through the unsheltered uplands. Around them roam argali sheep and wolves, while underfoot are chubby marmots, pikas, and darting hares. Rare Pamir mammals include snow leopards, bears, and the noble Marco Polo sheep, whose huge curling horns grow up to five and a half feet in length.

Tian Shan

Kyrgyzstan, China Rolling in a gentle arc for more than 1,500 miles from western Kyrgyzstan across China's Xinjiang region are the Tian Shan, Central Asia's Celestial Mountains, impressive in glittering might as they rise above some of earth's fiercest deserts.

Tian Shan peaks and other terrain, alpine in appearance, have steep, jagged ridges and clinging glaciers perched high up. Lakes lie in meadows surrounded by sylvan slopes of conifer, birch, and ash. But unlike Europe's Alps, the elevations here are intimidating, averaging more than 13,000 feet. The central cluster of peaks, on the Kyrgyzstan-China border, claims the tallest, most striking summits: Peak Pobedy, or Victory Peak, at 24,406 feet and its neighbor, Khan-Tengri, an imposing rock-and-ice pyramid considered by many the handsomest of all.

The long, lofty mountain chain captures considerable rainfall on its western and northern sides, allowing for the growth of some 2,500 plant species, more than in any other desert range. Rivers and runoff from the Tian Shan drain into huge Central Asian depressions, watering oases far below. In eastern Xinjiang, waters from the Bogda Shan, at an elevation of nearly 18,000 feet, fall in a dizzying descent to 500 feet below sea level, giving life to the populous Turfan Depression.

Throughout the sweep of the Tian Shan, above the desert floor, are steppelands; Turkic Uighurs and Kyrgyz inhabit these grassy seas.

Ussuriland

Russia At the far edge of northeast Asia exists a continental nook, bordered by the Sea of Japan and the great Ussuri and Amur Rivers, above the point where Russia, China, and North Korea come together. Its outstanding geographic feature is the north-south running Sikhote-Alin Mountains, a range more than 600 miles long, with few humans.

Miraculous Ussuriland harbors plants and animals from the Siberian north, China's temperate forests, and even from subtropical Southeast Asia. This rich, unexpected mixture has come about for several reasons: The maritime pocket escaped the last ice age, allowing many species to find refuge in such northern latitudes; Pacific monsoons moderate the climate while bringing plentiful rains; and river valleys and north-south ranges have helped channel species into the region.

Northern coniferous forests mix with birch as they sweep down to valleys and coastal cliffs, but in Ussuriland's south magnificent stands of oak, maple, ash, linden, and cork create an intensely varied broadleaf zone. Here are the Chinese soft-shelled turtle, Russia's only such turtle, and the gray goral, a diminutive goat-antelope with relatives in distant Burma and Kashmir.

More than half of Russia's bird species are represented in this avian paradise. Three species of endangered

KARST FORMATIONS, IRIAN JAYA

FERNS GROW TO GIANT SIZE IN IRIAN JAYA

cranes gather to mate in the Khanka Basin. Drongos, minivets, and flycatchers add a tropical flair.

The Siberian tiger, world's largest cat, stalks Ussuriland in search of boar and deer. Under intense pressure from poachers—responding to Asia's demand for animal parts as medicines—perhaps only 200 tigers remain in the wild. Even more threatened is the Amur leopard, clinging to existence with fewer than 30 individuals in Russia.

Wolong Natural Reserve

China The Qionglai Mountains, abutting Tibet's high plateau, contain a steep, misty preserve of lush terrain, home to the giant panda. Approximately a thousand wild pandas survive in three Chinese provinces, but Wolong in Sichuan, established in 1975 with 770 square miles, is their best single hope. Much of the reserve is dense forest cut by swift streams, a rich ecosystem with nearly 100 mammal species, 230 bird species, and 4,000 different kinds of plants. Riots of rhododendrons erupt each spring throughout a landscape of dark green deciduous trees, conifers, and gentle green bamboo.

Pandas rely almost entirely on arrow and umbrella bamboo, consuming 30 pounds per day as they ramble through the cold, wet foliage between elevations

of 5,000 to 11,000 feet. They share this domain with other rare and endangered animals—golden monkeys, red pandas, snow leopards, and flamboyant Chinese monal pheasants. Exceptional flora include Pére David's dove tree, whose pure white double bracts create the image of a tree full of alighting doves.

Wolong's breeding station seeks to understand panda habits and tries to introduce cubs into the wild. The preserve struggles to hold at bay logging roads, deforestation, and ceaseless population pressure.

Sundarbans

India, Bangladesh An ever wet region of forests and saltwater swamps, the Sundarbans wilderness area runs for 160 miles along the edge of India's West Bengal state and southern Bangladesh, at the head of the Bay of Bengal. Formed by the mouths of the Ganges, the Brahmaputra, and the Meghna, this maze of rivers, streams, and estuaries surrounds thousands of verdant islands. One of the world's largest mangrove forests provides rich nutritional material for a range of wildlife—crabs, shrimp, fish—all part of a complex food chain. Eight species of kingfisher hunt the vast swamp, an area for migrating and wintering birds.

Twenty varieties of mangrove

dominate this salty realm, where twice each day tides submerge the flats. Here are Gangetic dolphins, three species of otter, three species of wildcat and five species of marine turtle. Sundarbans crocodiles patrol swamps that protect the last Bengal tigers. About 350 of these powerful felines survive here, fully at home in the watery habitat, where they prey on boar, axis deer, and smaller animals. The Sundarbans Tiger Reserve in India (a thousand square miles) and three Bangladeshi sanctuaries offer some protection.

Serious threats to the wetlands come from human encroachment, cutting of fuelwood, overfishing, oil pollution, siltation, salinity from diversion of river water, and destructive cyclones.

Irian Jaya Highlands

Indonesia A great ice spine of frozen mountains and glaciers just below the Equator runs the length of New Guinea, world's largest tropical island. Its western half, Indonesia's huge province of Irian Jaya, is home to one of Southeast Asia's last strongholds of biodiversity. Eighty-five percent of the land remains a pristine wilderness of rain forests and mangrove swamps, with many parts still unconquered by explorers. Lorentz National Park, nearly the size of New Hampshire, rises from sun-drenched coasts to Puncak Jaya, Indonesia's tallest mountain at 16,024 feet and highest peak from here to the Himalaya.

Astounding avifauna marks Irian Jaya, especially the outlandishly plumed birds of paradise. Comical flightless cassowaries, with bright blue necks, red wattles, and horned helmets, eat large pebbles to help digestion. Outsize birdwing butterflies of arresting greens and yellows glide through forests on 12-inch wings. Unique mammals include nearly 50 marsupial species.

Irian Jaya's tribes now face modern invasiveness. Loggers and miners have arrived in force to extract vast untapped resources for world markets.

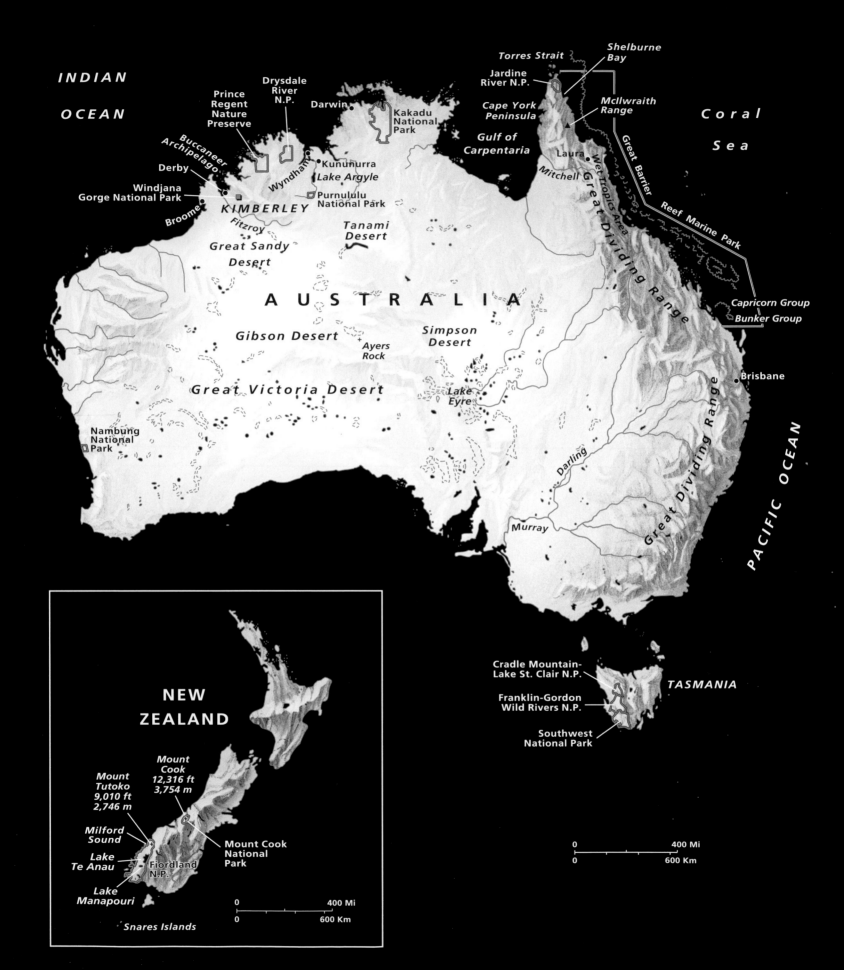

Australia

by David Yeadon

For all its urban patina and g'day-mate bonhomie, this four-billion-year-old worn stump of a continent remains a mysterious and elusive place. The vast majority of its 18 million inhabitants cluster like limpets in glass-tower and freeway-laced coastal cities perched on the edge of an almost three-million-square-mile land-mass that floated like a lonely ark from its Gondwanaland origins more than 65 million years ago. Its isolation spawned a host of unique plant species and endemic marsupial oddities in the form of kangaroos, potoroos, wombats, bandicoots, pademelons, and Tasmanian devils, along with that bizarre monotreme, the duck-billed platypus. The bulk of this red, dry, and eroded island is virtually empty from a human standpoint, known only to scat-tered remnants of Aboriginal groups, sheepherders, miners, farmers, and hardy cattle ranchers who somehow manage to raise their wide-roaming, semiwild herds on million-acre cracked- and scorched-earth ranches nearly devoid of vegetation.

Australia is a land still being explored and discovered. Among its wilder places, only Ayers Rock, a remote monolith in the "Red Center" of the country, attracts hordes of visitors. Most come to make the 1,142-foot climb to the rock's summit, much to the chagrin of local Aboriginal groups who consider Ayers Rock a sacred site. Fortunately the Australians themselves are now discovering the continent's enormous diversity and ecological wealth, and have developed an interest in studying and conserv-ing much of its natural heritage and wild places, and in returning tribal lands to the Aborigines for safekeeping. While inevitably there are problems and challenges ahead, Australia, along with richly endowed New Zealand, seems intent on setting high standards of conservation and ecologically sustainable land development that the rest of the world would be wise to evaluate.

Kimberley

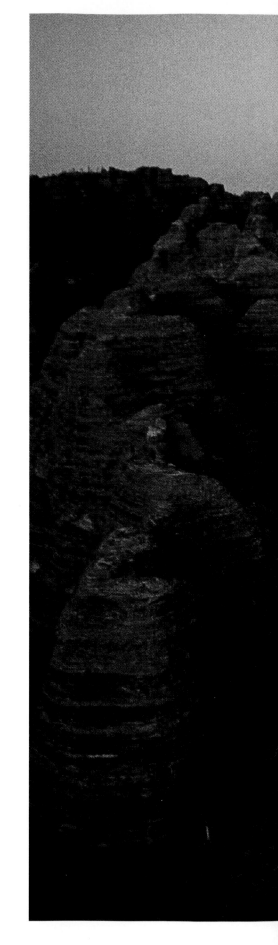

In the mid-1800s early explorer-dreamers entered this "land of distances and savage charm," eulogized the far northwestern Kimberley region as "luxuriantly grassed and watered," and heartily recommended it to neophyte pioneering families as ideal sheep-rearing territory. Gullible settlers should have heeded the words of buccaneer William Dampier, thought to have been the first English explorer of this wild coast in 1688, who declared it "not fit for a dog to live in." Instead, they dragged their way here through the unforgiving outback bush, where summer temperatures higher than 120°F sear the soul and spirit. They had battled nomadic Aboriginal inhabitants determined to protect their nearly 50,000-year-old homeland, Wandjina, named after its mythical inhabitants, the Dreamtime water spirits seen in many rock paintings in the region. The wild land they fought for was largely a vast red- and ocher-colored plateau edged by 360-million-year-old limestone reefs, dry, cracked, and broken. Here only flinty-leafed scrub, hardy eucalyptus, boab trees with their own self-sustaining reservoirs of water in their trunks, and such uniquely Australian life-forms as wallaroos, echidnas, dingoes, and frilled lizards could hope to survive.

In later years more comprehensive surveys of this 125,000-square-mile region did in fact reveal large portions of the Kimberley as suitable for sheep, cattle, and agriculture. The manic gold rushes of the 1880s and 1890s brought rampant if fleeting prosperity. Despite enormous tidal variations of more than 35 feet and the furious annual monsoon rains, or "wets," of January to March, the coastal settlements of Wyndham and Derby developed as key supply centers and, by 1910, Broome was renowned as the pearling capital of the world. In the 1960s the Ord River Irrigation Area and man-made Lake Argyle, Australia's largest freshwater lake south of the new town of Kununurra, created vast new agricultural resources despite environmental problems. The region also appeals as a prime bird-watching site for pelicans, galahs, honeyeaters, and ibis.

Yet despite the nibblings and nudgings of development over the last century, the Kimberley remains one of Australia's most evocative regions. Its landscapes range from the golden spinifex plains rolling south to the Great Sandy Desert and the boab- and termite mound-dotted

Wind and water carve beehive-shaped buttes, tight gorges, and soaring cliffs in the Bungle Bungle Range. Sculpted over 350 million years by seasonal rains and flash floods, this unique complex of banded sandstone towers is only one of the region's many remote and mysterious landscapes.

Wandjina figures float like clouds in Aboriginal art found on cave walls near the Gibb River. Unique to the Kimberley, the paintings represent the Dreamtime beings of sky and sea who brought rain and fertility to earth. These myths are key elements of an ancient culture celebrated in "corroborees," rituals of song and dance. Participants adorn themselves with body paint in traditional patterns (opposite).

plains of the west, to the vine thickets of the Mitchell Plateau, and the tidal rivers and creeks of the northern coast, home of saltwater and fresh-water crocodiles.

This is "The-Land-of-Wait-a-While." Australians are not generally known for their reticence but those who live here speak respectfully of "Kimberley Time," acknowledging the dominance of nature's power and rhythms over a still relatively unexplored land. Swirling, tidal wave-like floods erupt on the Fitzroy and other rivers during the "wets" and rage unchecked across a cracked and drought-plagued landscape. One of the

Kimberley

most uniquely eroded areas is the Bungle Bungle, Australia's exotic natural wonder on the eastern edge of the Kimberley in the 805-square-mile Purnululu National Park. "It's like no other place on earth," visitors gasp as they hike into its western canyons, barely body-wide in places, and take helicopter flights over its maze of sandstone and silica beehive-shaped hills, eroded by wind, rain, and floods into a lost-world fantasy landscape.

The rugged and fragmented Kimberley coast north of Broome is another world apart. From the several hundred islands and reefs of the Buccaneer Archipelago, fishing grounds of the Bardi Aborigines, along coastline hills flanking drowned riverbeds, through the coastal mangrove barriers and the pindan (a complex vegetation association of eucalyptus, acacias, and boab trees), and up into tidal rivers where 16- to 18-foot-long salt-water crocodiles hunt with protected-species abandon—you begin to sense the remarkable variety of scenic and ecological complexities that characterize this region. King Cascades in the Prince Regent River Nature Reserve tumbles in translucent filigrees down a 160-foot-high cliff, lush with hanging ferns. This reserve, a pristine area unchanged since pre-European times, has been established for strict conservation purposes with extremely limited access. Drysdale River National Park, where more than 600 plant species have been identified, is open for recreation, though difficult to get to.

While Broome, with its superb 13-mile-long Cable Beach, and other towns are rapidly developing their panoply of tourist attractions, the Kimberley still remains one of Australia's most enigmatic regions, rich in Aboriginal cultural heritage and ideal wild territory for inner-journey explorations of the spirit as well as more physical adventures in a true "last wild place."

Aboriginal Art

The art of the Aboriginal inhabitants of this vast continent illustrates the myths of a 50,000-year-old culture and tells of an unformed world shaped by ancestral beings—giant kangaroos, lizards, snakes, sea creatures, and witchetty grubs—during the Dreamtime of creation. The Aborigines today, who number more than 250,000 throughout Australia, see themselves as direct descendants of these beings and have the eternal responsibility of perpetuating the creators' dreaming tracks, or "songlines." Much of their art has been expressed in manifestations of these Dreamtime beings in cave paintings, along rock walls, on bark, and more recently in popular commercial forms. These are mystical and powerful works, filled with the timeless certainty of ancient beliefs and laws that gave social cohesion to these nomadic peoples.

Adaptability and endurance are vital to survival in the Kimberley's harsh climate. The goanna, a monitor lizard (right), can exist in a wide range of habitats including sedge-land, desert, and moist forest. On the tidal mudflats of Cambridge Gulf near Wyndham, the King River (below) nurtures mangrove trees, which in turn support a rich array of fish, birds, and animals.

Kimberley

Coral Reef

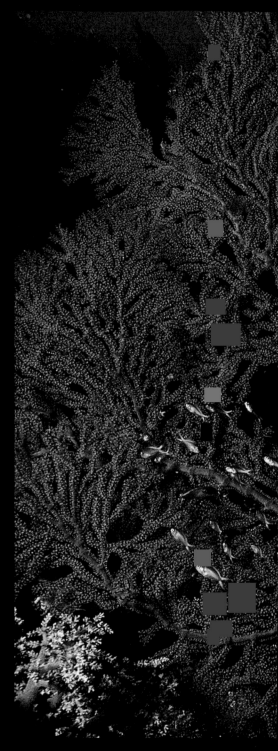

There are few experiences in life more exhilarating than floating in weightless limbo among the countless living organisms of coral reefs, embraced by a myriad of multicolored, polka-dotted, and striped fish in an environment inhabited by whales, manta rays, sharks, dolphins, barracuda and, in Australian waters, huge and friendly sweetlips.

These amazing, slow-growing, and fragile reefs are found primarily in tropical seas and the warm currents of temperate waters, and they provide shelter, food, and breeding havens for at least 25 percent of all marine species—as many as half a million different types of fish, crustaceans, worms, mollusks, and echinoderms. They are highly complex living ecosystems created by soft-bodied, sea anemone-like polyps that feed on plankton and other suspended organic matter, encase themselves in limestone, and add their collectively bonded and calcified remains to the ever changing "reef-creature."

Several basic reef types exist in the ocean, including fringing, barrier, atolls, and patch. Fringing reefs—the most widespread form—edge the shorelines of continents and mountainous islands, protecting them from storms and pounding waves that cause destructive erosion. Barrier reefs, the largest of which is Australia's 1,250-mile Great Barrier Reef, occur farther out in the ocean, separated from the shore by channels or lagoons, and grow most rapidly on their seaward side where oxygen and plankton are most plentiful. Other renowned barrier reefs include the Papua New Guinea, Fiji, Belize, and Bahamas reefs. Atolls are ring-shaped reefs surrounding a central lagoon and often form on the summit of submerged volcanoes. Patch reefs are usually fairly flat and circular, mapping the irregularities of the sea floor and existing independently of a reef formation.

Reef forms, the most diverse of which are found along the junction of the Indian and Pacific Oceans, possess highly delicate ecosystems dependent upon a subtle symbiotic recycling of nutrients in which each species plays a distinct role. Any disruption of this system can have dramatic repercussions on reef formation and durability. Global and oceanic warming, tourism and related coastal development, and coral mining are contributing to the declining health of reefs worldwide. Other threats include pollution, fertilizer runoff, excessive river sedimentation, souvenir-hunting, and overfishing.

Oceanographers estimate as much as 10 percent of the earth's reefs have been degraded beyond recovery and that a further 30 percent are likely to be lost within a couple of

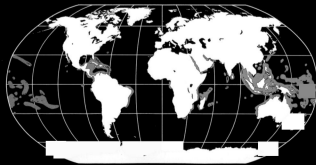

■ **Coral reef**

decades, particularly in the Caribbean region. The increasing popularity of the world's reefs may very well be the primary cause of their ultimate annihilation—a dilemma shared by many of the earth's wilder places. About 300 reef areas are currently protected, and almost 600 reef areas have been recommended for protection. Increased understanding of ecosystem dynamics and a coordinated and timely balancing of the competing demands of man and nature are the keys to mutual and sustainable survival.

Can our reefs survive? The exotic beauty of coral formations, such as these red gorgonian sea fans in the Bismarck Sea east of Papua New Guinea, is created by vast colonies of tiny polyps. Their survival is threatened on reefs worldwide by excessive tourism, coastal development, pollution, and a host of other destructive, man-created forces.

Bathed in the vibrant blues of the Coral Sea, Australia's Great Barrier Reef stretches over 1,250 miles along the Queensland coast and is composed of about 2,900 individual reefs, shoals ,and islets — almost all protected by a 135,000-square-mile marine park, the world's largest undersea sanctuary.

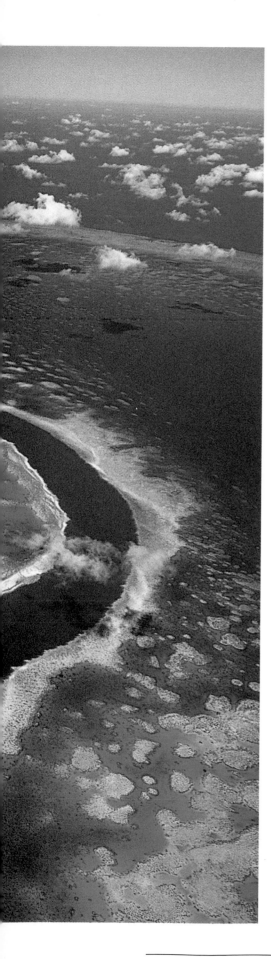

Great Barrier

"It is a Wall of Coral Rock rising almost perpendicular out of the unfathomable Ocean.... The Large Waves...meeting with so sudden a resistance makes a most Terrible Surf, breaking Mountains high...."
Capt. James Cook, 1770

The famous British seafaring explorer had every justification for his purplish prose. On June 11, 1770, James Cook's ship the *Endeavor* ran aground on this 1,250-mile-long reef and was saved by a skilled captain and a well-trained crew. After jettisoning their cannons and ballast to get off the reef, they finally managed to beach the ship in a small inlet where today's Cooktown now stands. A few years later, Capt. William Bligh, whose amazing 3,600-nautical-mile voyage in a small boat following the mutiny on the *Bounty* is still the stuff of legend, managed to sail through the reef safely and was later made governor of Australia's New South Wales for his troubles. Unfortunately, H.M.S. *Pandora,* which came to capture some of the mutineers on Tahiti, lost most of her crew on a reef wreck here in 1791. At least 30 wrecks of historic interest are known in the reef area.

An old sailor once claimed that "nobody can sail through Hinchinbrook Pass [a notorious reef hazard] and not believe in God." Today, more than a million annual visitors might claim equally mystical experiences through the very existence of the vast and beautiful Great Barrier Reef Marine Park. It covers about 135,000 square miles with a mosaic of some 300 islets, 618 continental islands, and more than 2,900 individual reefs, and boasts 1,500 species of fish, at least 4,000 species of mollusks (including giant clams weighing more than 400 pounds), more than 240 species of birds, and 400 species of coral. According to the world heritage site description it is "by far the largest single collection of coral reefs in the world. Biologically [it] supports the most diverse ecosystem known to man...provides some of the most spectacular scenery on earth...[and] provides major feeding grounds for large populations of the endangered species *Dugong dugon* [sea cows] and contains nesting grounds of world significance for the endangered...green turtle and loggerhead turtle."

Distinctly visible from the moon, this is the largest structure on earth built by living things—and still growing. Although it is one of the richest marine habitats on the planet, the reef's workings and many of its organisms still remain a tantalizing mystery to science. While the limey encrustations of coral are rock-like and permanent, only the surface veneer of three to sixteen feet is living material—an immense conglomeration of countless trillions of individual polyps, that rests on thousands of years' worth of skeletons of dead coral polyps cemented into a solid structure. Hard coral formations such as staghorn, brain, and mushroom, and soft colonies of "dead man's fingers," sea fans, and sea whips, provide the beautiful and ever changing underwater reef architecture that is home to fish,

Great Barrier

sponges, crustaceans, mollusks, echinoderms, tube worms, and algae.

It is the highly sophisticated cooperation of species that is one of the key features of the reef. This is an environment reflecting infinitely complex meshing of mutual needs and interdependencies, constantly seeking balance and harmony. Even the recent coral-eating plagues of the gluttonous crown-of-thorns, a spiny-legged starfish that has reduced some of the reefs to little more than coral rubble, may not be the ecological disaster it first appeared to be. New theories suggest that this is merely one more previously unnoticed cycle of reef-rejuvenation activity—a kind of underwater forest fire that eats away the older coral growth to make way for younger and more diverse species.

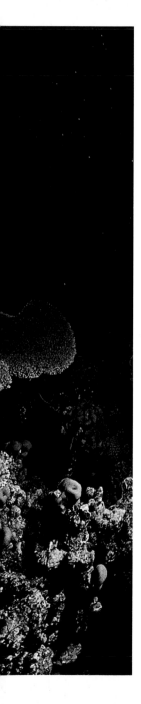

The reef, a relatively recent 8,000- to 10,000-year-old creation, which began its emergence on far more ancient reef remnants as seas rose following the melt of the last ice age, has three primary marine zones. The least disturbed northern part contains some of the most significant seabird colonies and turtle nesting sites in the western Pacific. Here, the waters are relatively shallow, less than a hundred feet deep; wall reefs form an almost continuous line at the edge of the continental shelf with only a few breaks in sheltered lagoons. The 150-foot-deep waters of the central section contain fringing reefs along the mainland, platform reefs, and many continental islands. The even deeper waters of the southern section are characterized by mazes of wall reefs and the rich corals and seabird nesting grounds on patch reef clusters such as the Capricorn and Bunker groups.

Seen from a small plane, the Great Barrier Reef is a whorled expanse of land and reef formations bathed by seas of every blue hue. From a boat one experiences the Robinson Crusoe appeal of seemingly untouched white coral sand beaches and idyllic wave-lapped havens, but underwater is where the true magic and boundless complexities of the reefs reveal themselves. On the outer eastern flanks one meets the free-wheeling, far-swimming marlin, tuna, and mackerel. Humpback whales come from Antarctica to calve in reef waters. Close to shore, endangered dugong feed in sheltered sea-grass beds. Around the reefs one enters a frenzied world of color and form—rainbow-hued, coral-munching parrot fish, clown fish, lizard fish, surgeon fish, groupers, barracuda, the many-lined sweetlips, and the huge 150-pound potato cod.

On the islands themselves the great brown

A large bommie of table coral (opposite, lower) offers sanctuary for a vast array of Great Barrier Reef creatures. Colorful reef denizens include a harlequin tusk fish (opposite, upper) that grazes lagoon floors crushing shells with its sharp *blue teeth; a canary blenny (above) finding shelter in coral crevices; and another unusual blenny-like fish (below) with three fins.*

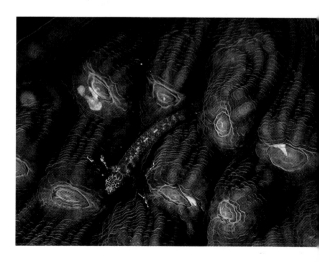

booby colonies of the Capricorn group and white-capped noddies of Heron Island draw visitors to Garden of Eden environments where they can walk among thousands of nesting birds that appear fearless in the face of intrusion. Forty seabird species, including the magnificent frigate birds with their seven-foot wingspans, have been recorded in the reef seas along with such colorful delights as red-tailed tropic birds.

But, despite marine park and world heritage site protection, all is not

A weary green sea turtle crawls laboriously back to her ocean home at dawn after ensuring the next generation. During the summer thousands of sea turtles come ashore on Great Barrier Reef beaches to create deep, secure, and warm sand-nests for their ancient egg-laying rituals. Each turtle deposits from 50 to 200 leathery-shell eggs, which release their tiny young (each weighing less than an ounce) in about eight weeks. The female must repeat the process regularly, laying as many as 1,000 eggs each season to offset the losses of her young to silver gulls, ghost crabs, and carnivorous fish.

perfect in paradise. The increasing popularity of the reef as a tourist attraction brings problems ranging from sewage disposal for hotels to reef damage by coral collectors and boat anchors. Runoff from agricultural pesticides and fertilizers, soil erosion, and river sediments can affect coral communities. The future will be, as in many of the earth's wild places, a constant challenge of balancing the demands of nature and of man. Here, at the Great Barrier Reef, the balance, so far, holds firm.

Mangroves and empty beaches await adventurous travelers at the northern extremity of Queensland's Cape York Peninsula, known locally as "The Tip." Jutting toward New Guinea, the peninsula became an ancient gateway for nomadic tribes who entered the continent more than 50,000 years ago.

Cape York

A "wild and strangely beautiful spike of land," the Cape York Peninsula is one of Australia's last frontiers. Split by the diminishing spine of the Great Dividing Range, this tip of northern Queensland, 400 miles long and 54,000 miles square, is a land of varied ecosystems and climatic extremes. Sweeping savanna, wetlands, rain forest, coastal sand dunes, and scrub all mingle in untamed splendor. During the "wet," the monsoon season from December to April, torrential storms bring 80 inches of rain, revitalizing coastal relics of the once vast ancient Indo-Malaysian rain forest. Rivers burst their banks and spread out, inundating huge areas of flatland. Then the floods gradually evaporate. During the dry season, seven months of withering drought, rainless lightning storms may set the bush ablaze.

The lowland rain forests of the east coast are of a type sometimes called monsoon forest, which mixes evergreens, such as laurels and palms, with deciduous figs and other trees that drop their leaves during the dry season. The forests are home to the six-foot-tall flightless cassowary, a relative of the African ostrich, and the endemic cinnamon antechinus, an insectivorous mouselike marsupial. Forest denizens also include rufous spiny bandicoots, spotted cuscus, and sugar gliders, opossums that "fly" between trees using parachute-like membranes between their front and back legs.

Fauna on the peninsula is remarkably diverse. There are 81 kinds of mammals (including more than half of the continent's bat species), 49 frog and 156 reptile species, more than 360 kinds of birds, at least 75 fresh water crustacean species, 47 spider and over 600 insect species, and, in the Jardine River more than 30 kinds of freshwater fish.

While the number of visitors increases each year, the resident population of the peninsula and the Torres Strait Islands to the north is sparse and includes around 7,000 Aborigines, who live in remote reserves and communities. Their ancestors crossed the ancient land bridge from New Guinea and Southwest Asia more than 50,000 years ago, and evidence suggests that this was once the most densely populated region of the continent. Records of early people's beliefs and activities still exist in the Quinkan Galleries, a series of open chambers near the town of Laura filled with 13,000-year-old rock paintings of dugong, crocodiles, and giant turtles—all creatures of the

Aboriginal Dreamtime stories, in addition to being valuable real-time food sources. One gallery boasts a 100-foot-long painting of almost 400 individual figures, depictions of sorcery practices, and strange animal forms.

More recent evidence of man's intrusions can be seen in the ghostly remnants of gold settlements and in the disturbance of east coast dunes by mining for silica sand. While the western plains have also suffered their share of exploitation in the form of bauxite and mineral mines and low density cattle ranching, they remain largely as early explorers found them.

While exploitation of the cape has been held in check by a combination of dramatic isolation, rugged topography, difficult climate, and the creation of nine national parks, more protection might be needed to ensure the future of one of Australia's most significant biogeographic regions. Although national parks cover an impressive 10 percent of the cape, such spectacular features as the silica sand dunes of Shelburne Bay are not yet included. Similarly, while only 2 percent of the peninsula is rain forest, the most notable region includes the undisturbed Hoop Pine stands located in the McIlwraith Range, 150 miles north of the world heritage Wet Tropics Area, which remains a timber reserve. Currently less than a quarter of the cape forests are protected, yet they contain the second highest concentration of rare and threatened plants of any rain forest in Australia.

While the cape's wild and pristine character appears enduring, new challenges of all kinds continue to arise. Prospecting initiatives around the Mitchell River catchment area threaten the Aborigines' subsistence fishing. Proposals have been made for the construction of a commercial space launch site on the west coast. Wilderness adventure offerings in the outback are on the rise and current tourist loads are increasing annually.

Massive buttress roots support towering trees in shallow soil in Daintree National Park (opposite). Exotic life-forms such as Boyd's forest dragon (left), delicate spider lilies (above), and tiny tree frogs with disked fingers and toes (below) enjoy a protected existence here in remnants of

Queensland's once vast tropical rain forests.

FOLLOWING PAGES: Constantly changing shoals are intriguing evidence of furious tropical storms and tidal erosion on Cape York's northeastern shore. Brown patches of color are created by tannin stains from coastal tea trees.

Recent public and media protests prompted a newly elected Queensland government to attempt to establish a nine-million-acre conservation zone for the east coast of the peninsula. Conservationists hoped to create one of the finest national park systems in the world's tropical savanna zone, but a change of government put the plan on hold. Whether Cape York Peninsula will survive as one of Australia's most scenic and ecologically varied last frontiers remains in doubt.

Fiordland
New Zealand

Across the vast and magnificent reaches of New Zealand's Fiordland National Park, one can be so overawed by the startling power and beauty of these glaciated mountain ranges, crystal clear lakes, and deeply incised fjords that some of the subtle signs of man's intrusions may not be so immediately obvious. But significant ecological damage was done here—by Maori hunters who arrived from Polynesia probably in the 10th century, and by 18th- and 19th-century European visitors who introduced dogs, rats, stoats, pigs, and other predators that destroyed many of New Zealand's endemic bird species. Evidence suggests that the ground-dwelling takahe, previously thought to be extinct, still has a resolute beakhold on life in the remoter Fiordland regions, and one of the world's largest parrots, the kakapo, still survives on offshore islands. Herds of red deer, a major threat to fragile alpine vegetation, are being actively reduced in line with a park policy to mitigate the impact of exotic introduced species.

Compared to the pastoral expanses of New Zealand's northern sheep-dotted vales and plains, Fiordland is a majestically crumpled wilderness. Thrown up by the heavings of the Pacific and Indian-Australian tectonic plates to form a maze of mountains, Fiordland was scoured and gouged by Ice Age glaciers and, following the last melt around 14,000 years ago, flooded to form 14 classic Norwegian-type fjords. The most renowned is Milford Sound at the northern end.

Fiordland National Park protects 4,850 square miles of this magnificent region—nearly 5 percent of this small island nation—and the creation in 1990 of the South West New Zealand World Heritage Site encompassing three other national parks, has brought international recognition to this unique conservation area. Successful campaigns in the 1960s and 1970s restrained the hydroelectric industry and prevented the flooding of Lake Manapouri, one of a chain of beautiful lakes on the eastern edge of the park created by meltwaters dammed by glacial moraines and fed constantly by annual rainfalls of up to 150 inches. Strict policies including restrictions on the number of hikers, or "trampers," on the Milford Track and several

The misty majesty of Mitre Peak dominates southwest New Zealand's Milford Sound, one of the most popular destinations in the 4,850-square-mile Fiordland National Park and even larger world heritage site. This magnificent wilderness encompasses 14 great glacier-gouged, ocean-flooded fjords, contains more than 700 plant species, and is laced with 9 notable hiking and kayaking tracks.

A serene, forest-bound pool near Sutherland Falls (below) is typical of "tramping" delights found along Fiordland tracks. New Zealand's national symbol, the chicken-size kiwi (opposite), is a curious remnant of many types of flightless birds that evolved in the islands' once predator-free environments.

other notable tracks, coupled with the banning of intruders in three special areas, help ensure the preservation of this region.

Jagged, frost-shattered mountains—most notably Mount Tutoko (9,010 feet) and Mount Madeline (8,380 feet)—tower above the alpine zone of snow-tussock grasses, heath shrubs, and delicate clusterings of mountain daisies, Maori onions, and South Island edelweiss. Below the snowline, where some of the highest waterfalls in the world tumble hundreds of feet

Fiordland

into shadowy, moist lowlands, one enters the eerie beech forests filled with stunted trees, twisted and gnarled in a riotous tangle above a ground cover of mosses, liverworts, and ferns. The lower temperate rain forests are famous for their rimus, magnificent towering red pines, while the river flats of the glaciated U-shaped valleys are said to resemble the ancient swamp forests of the Mesozoic era.

Fiordland has over 700 species of higher plants, including some 20

that are endemic, but a single type of bat and scattered colonies of fur seals reflect the paucity of mammals both here and throughout New Zealand. For some reason, as the island landmass separated from Gondwanaland more than 70 million years ago, it was birds that became the dominant species.

For all its natural riches, Fiordland is an arduous place to explore, particularly along the ten-day Dusky Track and three-day George Sound Track. Attracted initially by blue-sky photos of peaks, lakes, and waterfalls, disgruntled trampers often find themselves plodding through cloud-bound scenery, dowsed in constant rain on mud-churned paths, sharing basic facilities in chilly huts, and following rigidly enforced hiking schedules on reserved tracks. Those preferring an easier overview of the region drive the 75-mile-long Milford Road, Fiordland's only highway, from Lake Te Anau— once home to a mythical "lost tribe" of Maori—to the tight cleft of Milford Sound, where the smoothed rock walls of 5,550-foot-high Mitre Peak create the world's highest sea cliffs.

Despite the tough terrain and climate here, few return untouched by the power and pristine glories of this remarkable corner of the globe.

Flightless Birds

For islands that could boast only a couple of bat species as native land mammals when early settlers arrived, New Zealand's bird population at that time consisted of a remarkable 250 distinct species living in something approaching idyllic harmony. A wide range of flightless birds emerged in an environment free of mammalian predators, including some 20 species of the almost mythical moa. Human intrusion brought rats, cats, dogs, and other alien mammals, along with environmental despoliation that within little more than a century eradicated a host of endemic species, particularly the defenseless flightless birds. Only four species remain: the very rare and carefully protected takahe and kakapo, the inquisitive weka, and three types of long-beaked kiwi, New Zealand's national emblem.

FOLLOWING PAGES: Alpine vegetation on Mary Peak above dramatic Caswell Sound is among the many distinct habitats found in this "Switzerland of the South Pacific"— which is also renowned as one of the wettest places on earth.

Other Wild Places

Tasmanian Wilderness

Tasmania For such a moderate-size island of 26,380 square miles (less than one percent of Australia's landmass), Tasmania boasts a higher proportion of its territory as national parks and reserves than any other Australian state. By far the most impressive region is the 5,400-square-mile Tasmanian Wilderness World Heritage Area, which placed the state's three largest parks—Cradle Mountain-Lake St. Clair, Franklin-Lower Gordon Wild Rivers, and Southwest under UNESCO protection in 1982.

Untracked mountain and forest wildernesses seem to stretch forever in all directions. Many of Tasmania's unique plant species have close relatives in South America, and the southwest's temperate rain forest, renowned for its dense-canopied, 90-foot-high myrtle beech and almost impenetrable layer of low horizontal scrub, shares similarities with the fjordlands of New Zealand and Western Patagonia in South America. In the north and southeast, Tasmania's highest mountains, including Mount Ossa (5,336 feet), possess the columnar structure characteristic of a Jurassic dolerite plateau remnant. The central southwest Precambrian ranges date back well over 700 million years and have produced the glistening white quartzite flanks and peaks of Frenchmans Cap and Federation Peak. Eons of erosion have carved spectacular gorges along the Franklin and Gordon Rivers, where magnificent hundred-foot-high clusters of Huon pine can still be found.

The flooding of the Bass Straits between Tasmania and the Australian mainland following the last ice age led to the isolation of unique species of flora and fauna including the almost mythical thylacine or "Tasmanian tiger," thought to be extinct since the 1930s. Habitats of such exclusively Tasmanian creatures as the tiny 28-inch-high red-bellied pademelon, the Tasmanian devil, and the endangered orange-bellied parrot are conserved under world heritage status.

Kakadu National Park

Northern Territory By world heritage site and national park standards this is about as good as it gets in Australia. One hundred miles from Darwin, capital of the Northern Territory, this pristine 7,825-square-mile, New Jersey-size region, one of the world's largest national parks, encompasses several complete ecosystems and an entire drainage basin from source to coast. In addition, Kakadu boasts an outstanding gallery of Aboriginal art, chronicling their 40,000-year history here along an 800-foot-high, 300-mile-long sandstone escarpment. The region comprises an extensive range of tropical habitats including coastal mangrove swamps, eucalyptus forest, small pockets of rain forest, and floodplains and billabongs filled with waterfowl particularly during the May-September dry season. More than a third of Australia's bird and plant species and a quarter of its freshwater fish species reside here, unmolested by the invading animal and plant species that plague other parts of the continent.

Almost one-half of the park is owned by Aboriginal people, some of whom still live a traditional lifestyle, hunting and fishing in remote sectors. Others work as park staff interacting with more than 200,000 annual visitors to this uniquely unspoiled region.

Simpson Desert

Central Australia Set in the harsh, barren center of the continent, the 58,000-square-mile Simpson Desert possesses a timeless beauty in its unrelenting sand dune ridges. Rippled across an ancient seabed drained by cataclysmic upheavals about 60 million years ago, some dunes are as long as 125 miles. Shallow claypans, serpentine lines of vegetation marking dry creek beds, and the vast, eye-searing whiteness of the Lake Eyre salt flats in the south, provide the primary features in these endless parallel pleats of sand. Great plains of red, ankle-snapping "gibber" somehow support a gray-green

veneer of flesh-piercing spinifex scrub and stunted mulga trees, both of which have developed innovative ways of collecting and conserving scarce water from annual rains of less than five inches. Summer temperatures rise over 120°F. During the day all seems dead and silent in this landmark-less desolation, but cool nights bring a frenzy of activities by snakes, kangaroo rats, goannas,. geckos, lizards, beetles, scorpions, and centipedes. Adaptation and patience are the keys to survival here: Some frogs carry internal supplies of water and bury themselves until the rains come; marsupials store food reserves in unusually fat tails; short-lived creeks and water holes release myriads of freshly hatched fish after sudden downpours, when wildflowers appear miraculously; and birds species such as wood swallows and zebra finches fling themselves into a flurry of instant breeding. The ephemeral

SOUTHWEST NATIONAL PARK, TASMANIA

SUMMIT OF MOUNT COOK AT SUNSET

lakes draw a sudden profusion of galahs, budgerigars, herons, kites, and gray teals—and then it's back once again to the unrelenting heat, when everything sleeps and waits.

Nambung National Park

Western Australia From the air all you see are vast stretches of desolate coastal dunes, but closer inspection reveals thousands of golden, intricately shaped limestone pinnacles ranging in height from tiny pencil-like "twigs" to ten-foot-high monoliths scattered across the wind-rippled quartz sand.

Formed over more than 35,000 years by the slow calcification of lime, leached from the sand, around the roots of dune vegetation, the Pinnacles present one of Western Australia's most bizarre visual and geological anomalies. Surprising too in such a wilderness are the 100 species of birds, many easily observed in the 70-square-mile park. Emus and western gray kangaroos abound. Brush wallabies lurk in the thickets covering the ancient white Bassendean Dunes that lie inland beyond the dune heathlands, where kestrels hover and the stunted gum tree woodlands fringe the younger coastal dunes. Following the rainfall of about 25 inches between May and September, the park is transformed by wildflower carpets.

Snares Islands

New Zealand Considered one of the subantarctic's most valuable seabird sanctuaries, the wild and isolated Snares Islands, hidden away more than 100 miles south of South Island's Fiordland National Park, are home to an estimated 6 million ground-burrowing sooty shearwaters, more than 60,000 Snares crested penguins, and three endemic species of small land birds. Battered by ocean swells and frequent storms, these 30 or so islands and rocks provide meager shelter in the form of stunted forests of giant tree daisy and tussock meadows. Only a handful of licensed crayfishers and small research expeditions spend time on the inhospitable Snares, which has enabled the huge bird colonies to flourish unmolested by man and introduced predators such as rats, cats, and dogs. Steep cliffs, treacherous seas, and a dearth of safe anchorages are likely to ensure the survival of these pristine sanctuaries well into the foreseeable future.

Mount Cook National Park

New Zealand While charting the magnificent west coast of New Zealand's South Island, Capt. James Cook noted the "prodigious height" of the coastal mountains and named them appropriately "The Southern Alps." The grand climax of these ranges, still rising as the Pacific and Indian-Australian tectonic plates grind and heave along the Alpine Fault, is 12,316-foot-high, jagged-spired Mount Cook, the nation's tallest peak (the one the Maori call Aoraki), surrounded by some 20 other sky-scratching, 10,000-foot summits. Swathed in permanent ice and snow that covers more than a third of the 270-square-mile Mount Cook National Park, these young crests, barely five million years old, rise abruptly from the tussock basins of Mackenzie Country—named after a local folkloric sheep rustler of notorious repute. Five extensive glaciers fill the upper reaches of the park's main valleys. It is a wild, harsh land almost devoid of forest except for pockets of totara and silver beech in the lower valleys, and renowned for furious avalanches—one of which reshaped the entire east face of Mount Cook in 1991. A gentler side of the park is found on the flower-strewn alpine uplands, where the Mount Cook "lily"—the world's largest buttercup—flourishes along with spiky wild spaniards, South Island edelweiss, and woolly pillows of "vegetable sheep" bunched across the high greywacke rubble. Although popular with mountain climbers, hikers, and skiers, the park offers an abundance of solitary experiences—a key prerequisite of truly wild places.

PINNACLES DESERT, NAMBUNG NATIONAL PARK

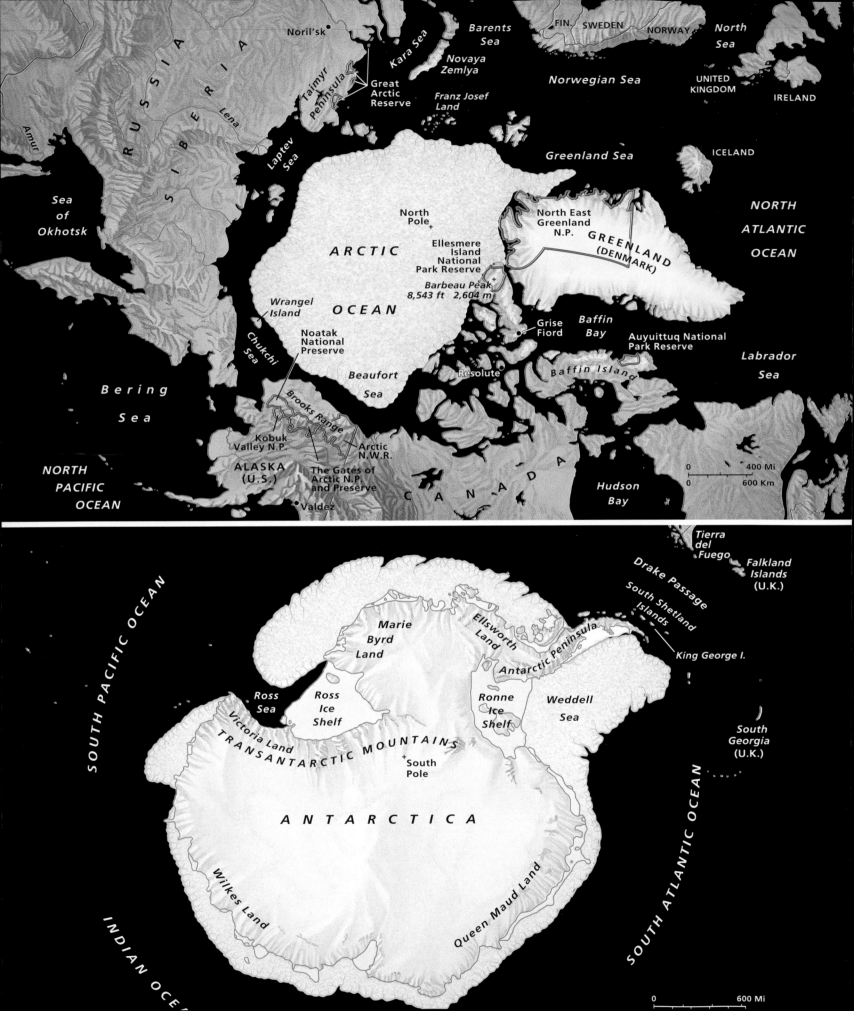

Polar Regions

by Michael Parfit
and Suzanne Chisholm

The polar regions are the extremes of the earth. Elsewhere in the world lands remain wild because of protective laws, but the polar regions are wild because they are so inhospitable. The Arctic and the Antarctic are the coldest, harshest, windiest, driest, iciest, and least-inhabited places on the planet. In winter, uninterrupted darkness shrouds these regions, which include parts of Alaska, Greenland, Siberia, and northern Canada and Europe, and all of Antarctica. Summers glow in constant sunshine, attracting flocks of migratory animals that come to feed and nest. These and indigenous species have adapted to the extreme cold.

To most beings, these vast, bone-chilling, wind-battered, treeless lands of mountains, ice, and rock are far from inviting. Antarctica is so coldly inhospitable that it has never had an indigenous human population. Temperatures as low as minus 126.9°F have been recorded. Summer brings some respite to the polar regions, but even then, the sun never rises high in the sky. In both regions, the white snow and ice reflect away as much as 95 percent of the sun's energy.

Antarctica is a mountainous land continent, smothered in ice up to two miles thick. Its polar opposite, the Arctic, is two-thirds ocean, covered by vast, semipermanent sheets of pack ice. In the polar regions, the oceans bring warmth, and life, to the coastal lands.

The adventure-hungry are drawn to the desolate Arctic and Antarctic. The landscape's splendid isolation, extreme harshness, and unspoiled beauty is captivating. Many return to these lands, seeking what the Antarctic explorer Ernest Shackleton called that "indescribable freshness...[which] must be responsible for that longing to go again and which assails each returned explorer from polar regions."

Antarctic Peninsula

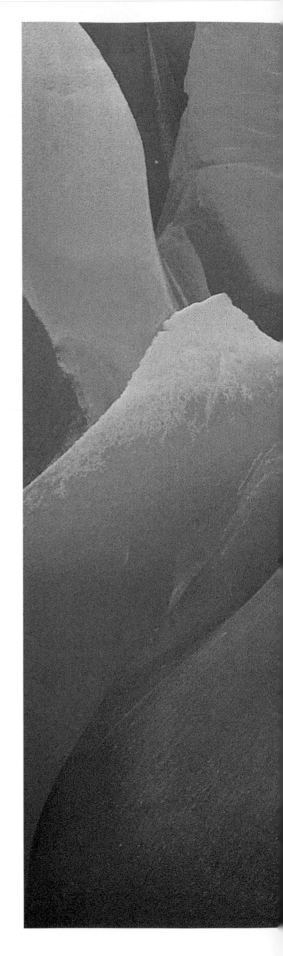

The Antarctic Peninsula, the most hospitable region of the last continent, is known as the "banana belt" of Antarctica. It's warmer, wetter, and more abundantly populated than the rest of the icebound landmass that occupies the "bottom" of the earth.

This 1,200-mile-long, mountainous peninsula protrudes north from Antarctica into the Southern Ocean, where the warming effect of open water allows some forms of life to survive. But things here are nevertheless fierce: Wind lashes the land; the average yearly temperature is below freezing; and animals—almost all connected to the sea in one way or another—must fight hard for food. Humans have never settled here, but today the exotic landscape attracts thousands of tourists.

The peninsula—whose northern tip lies 670 miles south of South America across the rough waters of Drake's Passage—was the first part of Antarctica to be discovered. A group of British and American seal hunters spotted the peninsula in 1820. Fur-seeking sealers flocked here in the 19th century, and whalers arrived in the 20th century. Today, two new waves of humans visit the peninsula for short periods of time: Scientists staying at research bases, and tourists from ships or planes. An increasing number of tourists adventure here, partly because it is the most accessible part of the continent. Some fly here, most landing at a long gravel runway on bleak King George Island, part of the South Shetland archipelago northwest of the peninsula proper. Most cruise here in luxury ships. They come to see clumsy penguins and graceful whales, turquoise ice cliffs, or the huge chunks of floating ice, which break off almost spontaneously from the continent and sail away to face their fate as icebergs at sea.

To help protect the fragile environment, the 43 nations party to a 35-year-old agreement known as the Antarctic Treaty recently approved a set of guidelines for environmentally responsible travel to Antarctica. The guidelines are stringent, because seemingly insignificant acts, such as disturbing wildlife by taking photographs, can be unexpectedly hard on

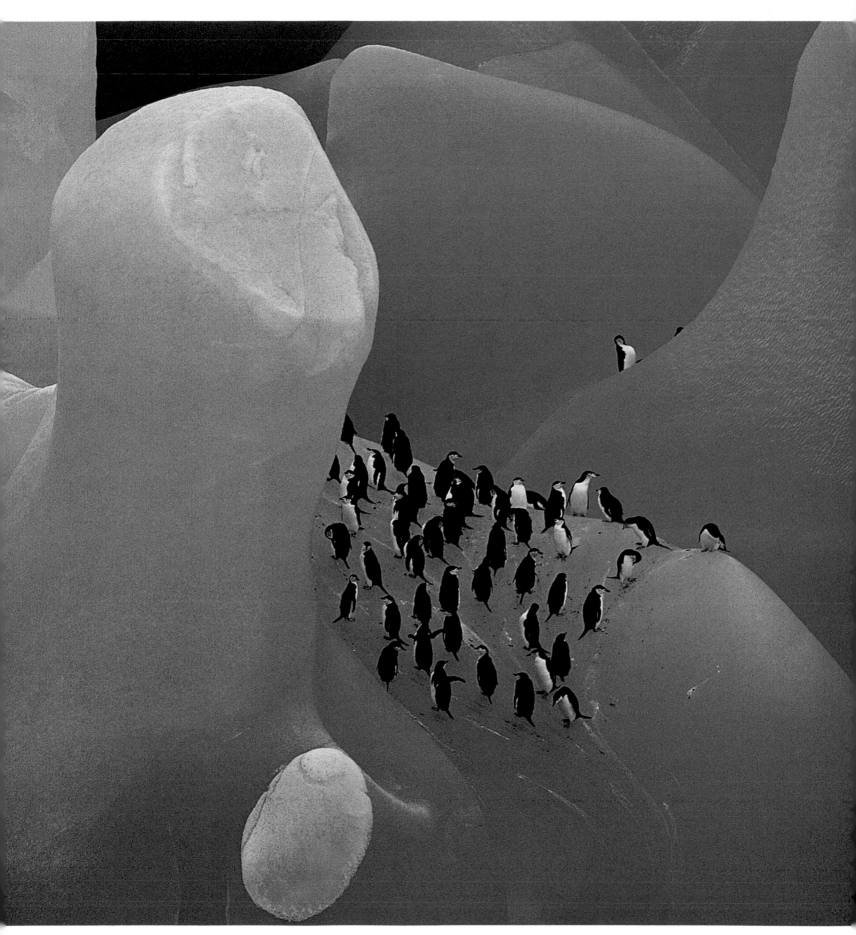

Having scaled the slippery incline on all fours, chinstrap penguins appear as tuxedoed passengers on a sapphire iceberg in the Weddell Sea. That life not only exists in Antarctica, but thrives, offers testimony to the wonders of adaptation.

an environment that evolved entirely without the human presence.

While only two percent of the entire continent is free of ice, two species of flowering plants—the Antarctic pearlwort and the hair grass—survive here; they grow on the west coast of the peninsula, where some snow manages to melt in the austral summer. Lichens and mosses, both undemanding in terms of water and soil requirements, thrive on rocks throughout Antarctica. The only land animals are resilient microbes and insects. During the summers, birds by the million migrate to the rocks of the Antarctic Peninsula. The flightless penguins come ashore to breed in huge, noisy, smelly colonies. Their offspring lie vulnerable to the predatory skuas that fly overhead.

Though Antarctica's landmass is visibly lacking life, its seas are bountiful, from the tiniest phytoplankton all the way up the food chain to the mighty killer whales. Crustaceous krill feed on the phytoplankton, and fish, squid, seals, penguins, seabirds, and whales eat the ubiquitous krill, which

Tourism has arrived in the Antarctic Peninsula (below). Passengers disembark expedition ships to cruise in small boats through a fantasia of icebergs, penguins, and seals. The experience is profound. Each austral summer (November to February) tourists visit penguin nesting colonies, and though tour companies police themselves with good intentions, disturbances to penguins and other wildlife are inevitable.

Antarctic Peninsula

gather to feed just below the water's surface during the summer.

Elephant seals can weigh up to 10,000 pounds, and are so round they appear to be made entirely of blubber. They swim to the islands off the Antarctic Peninsula to breed. The most common seals in the world, the crabeater, spend their lives on the Antarctic pack ice. Weddell seals can dive as deep as 2,000 feet, and venture as far south as the sea will take them. The rare Ross seals, the smallest of the Antarctic seals, are occasionally seen in the peninsula area. Leopard seals, the wolves of the south, weighing in at a hefty 700 pounds, swim the ice-strewn chilly waters, looking for penguins or small seals to feed on. Slender, swift fur seals, recovering in large numbers after being almost extirpated by hunters in the 19th century, can be seen frisking in the waves or sunning on rocks or icebergs.

Antarctica is cold by anyone's standards. But things may be changing. Temperatures on the Antarctic Peninsula have been rising. Over the past 30 years, summer temperatures have increased by about 4°F. The rising temperatures are due to global warming. The warmer temperatures are breaking ice shelves and melting the ice on the peninsula's coast. In 1995, a 50-mile-long iceberg broke away from the peninsula. One glaciologist has said the shelves of the Antarctic Peninsula are the warmest ice shelves in the world and are in "marginal existence."

Though the Antarctic pearlwort may be rejoicing at warmer weather, there may not be much cause for celebration: If Antarctica's entire ice cap were to melt, the earth's oceans would rise a couple of hundred feet, causing catastrophic flooding across the globe.

In the shorter term, the thinning of the ozone layer may pose a threat to life in the sea. If the sun's ultraviolet rays penetrate through the holes in the ozone layer, and enter the ocean, they may harm the phytoplankton, which are at the bottom of the marine food chain.

Other threats to Antarctica are overfishing and minerals extraction. Bountiful waters off the coast of Antarctica lure fishers with the technology to harvest great amounts of krill and fish. Some believe that oil and a wealth of minerals lie beneath the thick Antarctic ice cap, including gold, diamonds, and platinum. A moratorium on minerals extraction in Antarctica was signed by 26 nations in 1991, but whether this agreement will last as new extraction technology becomes available and as the world's energy demands rise remains to be seen. Yet the nations of the world had the foresight to protect Antarctica from nuclear proliferation with a treaty system ratified at the height of the Cold War; so they may continue to find ways to protect this cold, exotic, and wondrously wild place from short-sighted exploitation.

Calved from the great ice shelves that fringe Antarctica, icebergs are sculpted by the elements (above and following pages). The largest are comparable to Rhode Island and can be tracked by satellites should they drift into shipping lanes. Southern elephant seals (below) come ashore each year to mate and molt.

Penguin Gallery

Only the toughest can survive in frigid Antarctica. Penguins are cute, but they are also tough: They have warm blood, thick feathers, and can feed from the sea thanks to "supraorbital" glands, which allow them to ingest salty substances. Hopeless in the air and clumsy on land, these birds are fast and efficient in the water. Some can swim up to 25 miles an hour and can leap as high as 6 feet out of the water.

All penguins live in the Southern Hemisphere, although only two species are true Antarctic dwellers: the Adélie and the emperor. Adélies—named for a region of Antarctica—eat krill, fish, squid, and crustaceans; can stay at sea for six weeks at a time; and use the sun as a directional aid to find their way home. Emperors, which weigh about 65 pounds, are the most adapted to cold, huddling in colonies to stay

King penguin colony

Rockhopper penguin

Adélie penguin

warm. After laying a single egg, the female emperor goes off to sea for two months, while the male incubates the egg. Similarly, the male king penguin shares incubating duties, blanketing his partner's egg with his belly. Chinstrap penguins have a black line across their white throats, hence their name. Gentoos are recognizable by the white patches above their eyes, and are champion swimmers and divers. A final word of warning to visitors: Do not approach the aggressive rockhopper as he is likely to attack.

Chinstrap penguin

Gentoo penguin

Emperor penguin

Taimyr

utting out from north-central Siberia into frigid Arctic waters is the northernmost continental peninsula in the world, the Taimyr Peninsula. It lies entirely above the Arctic Circle, and is bounded on the west by the Kara Sea and by the Laptev Sea to the east. For three-quarters of the year, snow blankets this 150,000-square-mile land. Lakes are frozen from September to June, and temperatures as low as minus 50°F, worsened by strong winds, scare off most forms of life. From its southern boundary, the Middle Siberian Plateau, across the Byrranga Mountains, to the hilly plains on the rugged north coast, the desolate and remote Taimyr Peninsula is home to only the most rugged beings.

Despite its harsh climate, a variety of plants, animals, and people persist in living on the peninsula. Some species come to breed, some to search for food, and some to exploit. More than 200 species of colorful wildflowers, many of which are pollinated by robust and resilient bumblebees, grow in Taimyr in the summer. Migratory water-fowl from as far away as Australia fly here to build nests. Mining companies clamor for Taimyr's untapped mineral wealth, while environmental groups strive to protect its wildlife.

The first people to settle this barren land were the Samoyeds, who drifted to the Taimyr around A.D. 1000 from the south. The Russians arrived in the 16th century and presently account for 80 percent of Taimyr's population of 25,000. The indigenous population includes 5,000 nomadic Dolgans, descendants of the Samoyeds.

As in the rest of the Arctic, life emerges in the summer. The Taimyr Peninsula can be unusually warm compared to other Arctic wildernesses: Temperatures rise as high as 85°F; the average in July is about 45°F. The soil, paralyzed for much of the year in lifeless perma-frost—as deep as a thousand feet in some places—responds to this blast of heat by thawing for a few inches at the surface, turning the land into swamp. The Mongols named this land Siberia, which means "swampy forest." Swollen rivers twist their way through the undulating plains. Ground-hugging plants and a slew of colorful wildflowers peek out from the thin soil to embrace the permanent sunshine.

Living on the edge is a fact of life for hunter-fisherman Valeri Ryabkov, a self-reliant Russian resident of Taimyr who scouts for arctic fox and reindeer in his snowmobile. The sun creates a mirage of warmth, for Taimyr's northernmost point is the closest any continent reaches to the North Pole.

Northern Lights

Sometimes the vibrant nighttime skies in the Northern Hemisphere look as though children with paintbrushes had splashed their favorite colors across the heavens. These shimmering northern lights, or aurora borealis, can range in color from white to green to yellow to blue to red, and are often seen in the spring or fall. The auroras can appear as sheets, beams, arcs, patches, flames, or even coronas. They are caused by charged particles from the sun being deflected into the earth's geomagnetic poles. When the particles, which travel in streams, hit gases in the earth's ionosphere, they glow in the sky, often appearing as curtains. The aurora's color depends on altitude and the particles' wavelengths. White and green are the most common. As one moves farther north, the frequency of the auroras increases—the northern lights can sometimes be seen every day near the North Pole. Their movement is sometimes sedate, but sometimes almost violent: In the high darkness they swirl and flash, making the whole sky look wildly astir.

The 600-mile peninsula can be divided into three zones: the hilly coastal plains in the north; the Byrranga Mountains, which extend from the southwest to the northeast; and the vast, rolling North Siberian Lowland, which lies to the south of the Byrranga chain. In the most northern coastal region just a few mosses and liverworts can survive, but farther south, larch, spruce, low willows, and birch trees grow in the lowland tundra-forest. Larch is the only tree that can survive in permafrost, and is relatively abundant. Lichens, sedges, mosses, grasses, and tiny shrubs grow on the lowland plains, and the vegetation grows richer as one heads south.

A wide range of birds—waders, gulls, terns, swans, geese, and ducks—spends summers on the Taimyr Peninsula. Perhaps most notable is the striking red-breasted goose. About 10,000 of these rare birds fly from their winter homes in Romania to breed on the Taimyr tundra. Curiously, the goose is protected from the hungry arctic foxes by a symbiotic relationship with the usually predatory peregrine falcon. A goose builds a nest just a hundred feet from the falcon's nest. When a fox approaches, the goose honks loudly, and the falcon chases the fox away.

Roaming reindeer, which can weigh up to 700 pounds, love the tangled lichen cladonia, or reindeer moss, found in Taimyr. Up to 700,000 reindeer live here in one of the world's strongholds for these animals, known as caribou in North America. In early summer, great herds head north, seeking food and breeding grounds. Taimyr is also home to a small herd of musk oxen, sluggish and furry, recently reintroduced from North America. In the ice-filled waters off the coast of Taimyr, polar bears, beluga whales, seals, and walruses make their homes among the floes.

But these animals and their fragile environment are threatened, and not only by the hunters who are lured here. The rich stash of oil and minerals, including gold, copper, nickel, platinum, and uranium, attracts mining companies eager to explore and develop the terrain. Siberia is, according to some, the "cupboard" of Russia, with vast, unexploited minerals, an obvious temptation for the cash-starved Russian government. Sulfur gas from a huge nickel mine and smelter at Noril'sk, just south of the peninsula, effluents from Siberian pulp mills dumped into rivers that flow north through Taimyr into the Kara Sea, and contamination from a radioactive waste site, Novaya Zemlya, a few hundred miles away in the Kara Sea, all represent unchecked threats to Taimyr's wildlife and unspoiled wilderness.

In 1993, with the help of the Netherlands and the World Wildlife Fund (WWF), Russia set aside 14,500 square miles of the Taimyr Peninsula, including a Kara Sea archipelago, as the Great Arctic Reserve. Only the Dolgans and other indigenous tribes are allowed to live and hunt and trap inside the reserve. Some believe they may be the key to preserving this pristine Arctic wilderness. "Indigenous people," says Robin Pellew, a WWF director, "are the best conservationists."

Fishermen use reindeer (opposite), domesticated cousins of the caribou, to access traditional ice fishing areas on the frozen Bolshaya Polovinnaya River. The fish, a source of golden caviar, freeze almost instantly in the polar air. While summer finds Taimyr's tundra melting and flow- ering and filled with the songs of nesting birds, winter locks the land in a cold, dark vault, broken only by dancing northern lights and the pale disk of the moon (opposite and below).

Polar Desert

While images of parched landscapes, sun-beaten dunes, and camels may spring to mind when one hears the word "desert," the Arctic and the Antarctic, with their polar bears and penguins, are home to some of the world's driest deserts.

Deserts are characterized by minimal precipitation, arid land, and a short growing season, and precipitation in many parts of earth's wind-whipped polar regions averages only a couple of inches a year—less than in the Sahara. The little moisture that does fall from the sky becomes trapped away in ice or remains on the ground as snow. The key to releasing the moisture is heat, which can melt ice and evaporate water, but since the sun is absent from the polar regions for as much as six months a year, and never rises high in the sky in the long summers, most of the moisture remains frozen in glaciers, icecaps, or in the soil as permafrost. The frozen water is largely inaccessible to the polar plants and animals, that have acclimatized to these cold deserts.

Because summer Arctic temperatures often rise above freezing, some of the winter's snow and ice melts. Meltwater and the thawing of the upper few inches of permafrost provide some respite for arctic flora and fauna. The water, which does not drain away, creates marshes and swollen rivers, which provide sipping grounds for tundra plants and animals.

Arctic plants are subject not only to low levels of precipitation, but also to high Arctic winds, which evaporate precious moisture from their leaves. Many plants have adapted by developing small leaves, which reduce water loss. Some herbs have hairy, thick, or leathery surfaces that trap water and thus decrease the rate of evaporation. Some are succulent and can hold moisture. Most tundra plants grow very slowly and economize on water use. Some species, such as moss campion, have long roots that sustain the plant with a steady supply of water. Many species of tundra plants protect against dehydration in the winter by thickening their cells.

Despite these means of protection, plants in the Arctic hardly lead the comfortable lives of their counterparts in warmer regions. Willows, although trees, often grow only a few inches tall because of the harsh, dry conditions in which they grow. A 300-hundred-year-old willow may only be 3 inches in diameter. And 25-year-old spruce trees, just a foot high, are found in Alaska.

An average of about two inches of precipitation falls each year in eastern Antarctica, and scientists claim that in some places, rain hasn't fallen in two million years. The

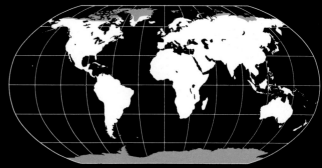

■ **Polar desert**

harshness of the dry and cold is compounded by fierce winds, which average 40 miles per hour. Few living beings exist on land; the largest land creatures are half-inch midges. Most of the visible life on Antarctica is vegetation. Only two species of wildflower are found. Lichens can remain dormant under periods of stress, and dehydrate themselves in the winter months to keep from freezing. And mosses grow huddled together in bunches that trap moisture and slow evaporation. In short, polar deserts, like those in hotter climates, are inhabited by life with a genius for adaptation.

The Danco Coast, on the west side of the Antarctic Peninsula, greets Gerlache Strait in a frozen salutation of land and sea. While water is abundant here, it remains locked away as ice and unavailable for plants and animals. It is the sea in Antarctica that supports life: phytoplankton (algae), zooplankton (krill), fish, penguins, seals, and whales.

Ellesmere

It seems hard to believe that the tenth largest island in the world has no permanent residents. There have probably never been more than a few hundred inhabitants over the centuries on this extraordinary island, the most northern of Canada's vast Arctic archipelago, the remote Ellesmere Island.

When you take a closer look, it's clear why: Life here is difficult. More than 40 percent of this 76,000-square-mile mighty island is covered in ice, and it is especially cold, even for the Arctic—in the summer, the average temperature is just above freezing. Getting here and getting around are prohibitively difficult. The main mode of travel between Ellesmere's three settlements—the Inuit village of Grise Fiord and two military bases—is by costly small airplane. And getting here from any major city in Canada is a longer flight than the distance between Los Angeles and New York.

Since the North Pole is just 475 miles from the northern tip of Ellesmere, some call the island "The Top of the World." But if it's the top of the world physically, it is also a pinnacle of natural beauty, ecosystem fragility, and isolation. The Canadian government established the 14,585-square-mile Ellesmere Island National Park Reserve on the northern part of the island in 1988, but has acknowledged that Ellesmere is not a place for social creatures: The government has called the island "one of the loneliest outposts in the world."

Paleoeskimos first crossed to Ellesmere from Siberia about 4,000 years ago. Their presence was intermittent, and anthropologists think they may have migrated north in search of musk oxen. Neoeskimos, or Thule culture Inuit, arrived 800 years ago from Alaska and stayed long enough to leave just a few artifacts. Repelled by the increasing cold of a changing climate, they soon headed south. In 1881, U.S. Army officer and explorer Adolphus Greely built Fort Conger on the northeast coast of Ellesmere.

The wilderness of Ellesmere may be cold and lonely, but it's not dull. It boasts the huge mountains of the Grant Land Range—Mount Barbeau rises to 8,633 feet—freshwater lakes, glacial rivers and valleys, plateaus, thick glaciers, a jagged coastline, and floe-strewn fjords. It even has a thermal oasis on the Fosheim Peninsula, Hot Weather Creek, where mountains block out cold weather from the northwest, and where average July temperatures can be 55°F, compared to 35°F hundreds of miles to the south.

Musk oxen stand shoulder to shoulder on Ellesmere Island. The Eskimo word for them, oomingmaq, means "the animal with skin like a beard." Adapted for life in the cold, musk oxen have guard hairs that reach 25 inches in length and thick underfur eight times warmer than sheep's wool.

Though Ellesmere is a polar desert, receiving just two and a half inches of precipitation a year, thawing soil and glacial meltwater nourish plants and animals during the sun-filled summers. On the south-facing slopes, where the sun's energy is reflected into the valleys, eager wildflowers—yellow arctic poppies, white heather, blue forget-me-nots, buttercups, purple saxifrage, and arctic blueberries—emerge to capture the sun's rays. Arctic hares, lemmings, Peary caribou, and hirsute musk oxen nibble at the lush grasses and sedges of summer. Foxes, wolves, and ermines roam in search of prey. The arctic tern, which makes a round-trip from the Antarctic each year, is just one of 45 species of birds, including ringed plovers, geese, ducks, loons, and gulls, which nest on the tundra. The hardy ptarmigan and the snowy owl remain long after the migratory birds head south. The coastal regions are also home to the king of the tundra, the polar bear.

Ellesmere Island National Park Reserve, located at the northern tip of the island, lies 375 miles from the village of Grise Fiord, one of Canada's northernmost communities. The reserve is protected from development and has become a great wilderness attraction to adventurers. Although hunting is not permitted in the park, and fishing is permitted only with a license, native Canadians retain their hunting, fishing, and trapping rights in the reserve.

The physical inaccessibility of Ellesmere Island, and the park in

Ellesmere

particular, has meant that only the most determined visitors experience this rugged natural stronghold. To get to Ellesmere you have to walk, snowmobile, or boat a long way, or you have to be wealthy. Park authorities point out that charters from Resolute to Lake Hazen in the park—a five-hour flight—can cost $20,000 ($13,560 USD), round-trip.

Once inside the park, the visitor can enjoy a truly unspoiled wilderness, hiking through river valleys, crossing glaciers, photographing polar bears, exploring the ancient campsites of the paleolithic peoples, or perhaps fishing for arctic char in Lake Hazen, Canada's northernmost freshwater lake.

The rise in tourism at Ellesmere Island is a potential threat to the wilderness, and possibly to indigenous peoples' lives. But another, less visible, threat looms: pollution from outside the Arctic, including oil spills, toxic chemicals, air pollution, heavy metals, and radioactivity.

The countries bordering the Arctic have pledged to protect it, under the Arctic Environmental Protection Strategy, a cooperative effort to address environmental concerns. But these threats are still minor and distant, and for now Ellesmere remains one of the most unspoiled of all islands in the world.

A fleet-footed Peary caribou (opposite), the smallest sub-species of caribou, dashes over spring snow on Ellesmere Island. Preyed upon by wolves, the caribou survive by delicate means balanced between high reproductive rate and high calf mortality. Caught in a reflective moment (above), an arctic wolf drinks on the shore of a summer lake. So thinly scattered are the animals they hunt—musk oxen, caribou, lemmings, ptarmi-gan—that each wolf pack needs approximately a thousand square miles of territory.

FOLLOWING PAGES: Undaunted by the vastness before it, a polar bear patrols the pack ice of Canada's high Arctic. Equally at home on ice, land, and in the sea, it finds a suitable world where we do not, following the freezing, shifting edges of opportunity and desire.

Brooks Range

The mighty and majestic Brooks Range slices through the sky like a 600-mile-long serrated knife, cutting off the North Slope of Alaska from the interior in panoramic style. Rising as high as 9,058 feet, the range is an extension of the North American Rockies. The northernmost continuous mountain range in the world, the Brooks Range lies entirely above the Arctic Circle.

The glacier-strewn array of peaks and valleys, which stretches from the Chukchi Sea to the Yukon Territory, is home to a variety of hardy wildlife, including lovely arctic wildflowers, an orchestra of songbirds, rare and once extirpated musk oxen, and huge herds of caribou. The uncommon beauty of the Brooks Range wilderness lures hikers and hunters in search of sport, isolation, and stunning scenery. These visitors' steps may place stress on the environment, but the North Slope is skirted by another valuable resource that attracts even more serious predators: oil.

Named for an early 20th-century American geologist, A. H. Brooks, the mountains, which are made of both sedimentary and igneous rock, have been repeatedly characterized by geologists as "mind-boggling." And if conservative scientists find the Brooks Range mind-boggling, so must the many nature lovers who have ventured to these mountains throughout history.

It is believed that the first band of paleolithic peoples crossed to northern Alaska from Asia 25,000 years ago. Since the Brooks Range is relatively close to their crossing point, the Bering Sea land bridge, it's likely some settled here. More recently, in the last few thousand years, Athabascan Indians and Nunamiut Eskimos, both caribou-dependent groups, settled in the valleys of the Brooks Range. Then, at the turn of the century, whalers, fur traders, and explorers appeared from the south and drove away most of the indigenous peoples.

The best-known professional explorer to have come to the Brooks was Robert Marshall. He first ventured here in 1929, and founded the Gates of the Arctic wilderness reserve, which is one of the four conservation units in the Brooks today.

Three-quarters of the pristine Brooks Range is protected in a network of such units: the 19-million-acre Arctic National Wildlife Refuge, the 8.4-million-acre Gates of the Arctic National Park, the 6.5-million-acre Noatak

Spokes of sunlight radiate across battlements of the Brooks Range. The northernmost chain of contin-uous mountains in the world, the range is largely protected within two national parks, a national preserve, and the Arctic National Wildlife Refuge, a total area of 35.6 million acres.

"Over these meagre lands they travel," writes biologist George Calef of the caribou (above), "obeying the commands of the seasons: the melting of snow, the budding of plants, the hatching of mosquitoes, the freeze-up of lakes and rivers." One of the world's greatest wildlife spectacles, the Porcupine Caribou Herd (opposite) travels every spring from Canada to the coastal plain of the Arctic National Wildlife Refuge, where cows give birth to their calves.

National Preserve, and the 1.7-million-acre Kobuk Valley National Park. Each of these preserves is remote, and a visitor can experience wildness in every sense of the word. Wild animals—grizzlies, caribou, sheep, wolves, coyotes, foxes, moose, musk oxen, and squirrels—roam the taiga (the sparse boreal forest) or the tundra, and bloodthirsty mosquitoes await overhead. Facilities are minimal or nonexistent, and there are no roads. Even hiking can be painstaking because of the endless masses of thick, gnarled tussocks of grass or tundra underfoot.

It is no surprise, then, that visitors choose to travel as the indigenous peoples and caribou have done for centuries, along the rivers. In the Gates of the Arctic, six wild rivers flow, swollen in the spring and summer months.

Brooks Range

These rivers—most designated as National Wild and Scenic Rivers—serve as the visitor's highways within the park. Canoes, kayaks, and rafts move the visitor with what one traveler described as "downright cushy" comfort through the mountains, to canyons, valleys, lowland forests, and pristine glacial lakes, where one can catch char, salmon, or grayling for breakfast.

And the Brooks visitor can expect the unexpected. The least-visited of the parks, Kobuk Valley, boasts an improbable, 25-square-mile "mini-Sahara" desert, complete with 33,000-year-old dunes, which can rise as high as a hundred feet.

Despite short summers, permafrost, and the aridity of the region, an impressive array of vegetation graces the Brooks Range each summer. The region south of the range is the taiga, where dwarf willow, alder, paper birch, aspen, balsam poplar, and white and black spruce grow amid sedges, grasses, lichens, and fireweed. North of the range, past the last spruce (celebrated with a sign), lies the tree-less tundra, where hardy and undemanding mosses and lichens rule. Once the constant sunlight of the Arctic summer arrives, tundra wildflowers—bluebells, purple saxifrage, lupines, cream-colored dryas, sweet peas, purplish-red Lapland rosebay, dark pink Kane lousewort, sunshine-colored avens, white heather, pink moss campion, blue forget-me-nots—blossom in a flurry of colors.

Perhaps the most impressive phenomenon in the Brooks is the semiannual migration of the caribou. Traveling in herds as large as 250,000, the caribou roam north in the summer to find food and to breed. One of the largest, the 200,000-strong Porcupine Caribou Herd, so-called because it winters in the Porcupine River basin, treks across the Brooks Range in the spring as far north as the coastal plain, where the calves are born.

Oil and Caribou

Touted as the "American Serengeti" because of the huge herds of migratory caribou that trek across it each spring, the Beaufort Sea coastal plain of the Brooks Range is also home to vast oil reserves. Some believe as many as nine billion barrels lie underground. Under provision 1002 of the Alaska National Interest Lands Conservation Act, 1.5 million acres of the lucrative coastal plain are unprotected. If oil companies drill, the calving grounds and the rich food sources of the 200,000-strong Porcupine Caribou Herd may be destroyed. And animals are not the only ones threatened. Thousands of indigenous peoples in Alaska and the Yukon have depended on the caribou for centuries for food, clothing, and shelter.

The light of high latitudes paints brilliant brush strokes of ochre, sienna, and cinnabar across a palette of Brooks Range foothills. South-facing slopes offer sun traps that produce warmth and lush summer willow growth where wildlife, such as a mother moose and her twin calves (opposite), can browse in preparation for the coming winter.

But the caribou aren't the only species drawn to the coastal plains north of the Brooks Range. The discovery of oil at Prudhoe Bay in 1968 led to the building of an 800-mile pipeline south through the Brooks Range to Valdez. Much more oil is believed to lie in the adjacent coastal plain. The potential oil exploration and development pressures on the Brooks Range wilderness have been mitigated by the fact that 35.6 million acres are

Brooks Range

The horizon-hugging sun casts perpetual, oblique rays on the Arctic during the summer months. The upper inches of the permafrost thaw, and thin soil nourishes hardy plants. The south face of the Brooks Range becomes much warmer than the north because the high mountains prevent some of the low-lying sun's energy from reaching the north face, essentially trapping the sun. Vegetation on the relatively balmy, sun-trapped south side of the mountain is richer. Arctic wildflowers burst into color during the short but intense growing season. Here, small trees and shrubs may grow as high as ten feet. The mountains roughly separate the forested taiga from the treeless tundra. Trees dwindle on the North Slope, where the rocky tundra begins, and the most common plants are lichens. Grasses, mosses, and sedges grow on the soggy tundra. But flowers bloom here, too. Sun-worshiping plants, such as avens, tilt toward the distant sun, trapping the precious rays of light.

protected as parks and preserves. But there is a loophole: Congress has set aside a one-and-a-half-million-acre, unprotected "study" region on the coast, under the Alaska Lands Act. Further development of the oil business in Alaska would certainly result in ecosystem damage, habitat displacement, the risk of spills, and other pollution. If drilling proceeds, the caribou will have to find another empty place to roam.

Other Wild Places

Baffin Island

Canada It's called the "Land that Never Melts." Auyuittuq National Park Reserve on Canada's Baffin Island lies just above the Arctic Circle and is smothered by huge glaciers. Temperatures can be bone-chilling. Snow can fall from the sky at any time of the year. Contrary to a general trend of global warming, some places in Auyuittuq may be growing colder.

The harsh climate of Baffin Island allows only the hardiest animals to survive. Sharp-hoofed barren-ground caribou have thick layers of fur that keep out the cold and attract Inuit hunters, who make coats from it. Arctic foxes are also wrapped in warm fur. And the mighty polar bears, which breed on the east coast of Baffin Island, have thick layers of both fur and fat to block out the cold Baffin air.

Boat, snowmobile, or helicopter are the only ways to reach Auyuittuq. Once in the park, the visitor travels by foot, skis, or perhaps dogsled, and revels in

WANDERING ALBATROSS ON SOUTH GEORGIA ISLAND

the scenery. Rivers pound through the valleys, long fjords reach inland like crooked fingers, and rough mountain peaks, embraced by glaciers, rise to 7,000 feet. The tundra is splattered with butter-colored arctic poppies, pink willow herbs, purple saxifrage, and creamy white cotton grass; and brilliant aquamarine lakes provide evidence that glaciers have been here recently, while lush valleys offer unparalleled opportunities to see snowy owls and lemmings.

Wrangel Island

Russia Isolated in the chilly Chukchi Sea almost 90 miles north of eastern Siberia, surrounded by imposing sheets of pack ice, and abused by ferocious winter gales, Wrangel Island seems an unlikely wildlife refuge. But this 93-mile-long, 78-mile-wide mountainous island is home to several animal and plant species, and has been designated an international biosphere reserve.

The Arctic summer sun melts away the winter snow, uncovering the lowlands and mountains. Wrangel Island, despite its latitude of 71°N, has neither glaciers nor a permanent icecap. Rocky coastal cliffs and ice-free plateaus draw unique species of birds here to nest, including rare breeding sandpipers and 65,000 snow geese from the United States. In total, more than 500,000 birds flock to the bountiful Wrangel coast each summer.

The persistent summer sun also manages to loosen some of the coastal ice, opening swimming paths for walruses, seals, and mighty polar bears. As many as 80,000 walruses breed on Wrangel, making it among the most important breeding places in the world.

Up to 300 polar bears den on Wrangel, which gives it the highest density of polar bears worldwide. Only the females hibernate, often giving birth under the snow to twins, which wait until spring to peek out at their island world—a place inhospitable to most, but a refuge and home to them.

DEEP FJORDS CONTAINING LARGE ICE FRAGMENTS, GREENLAND

South Georgia

United Kingdom South Georgia Island lies 800 miles east of the Falkland Islands, like a stone dropped in the Southern Ocean as if by accident. James Cook first discovered the isolated 1,450-square-mile, wind-whipped island in 1775, and staked Britain's claim to it. It is cold and forbidding: A small British Antarctic Survey station is the only sign of human life. Snow falls at least 180 days each year, and three-quarters of the island is buried in permanent snow. The island is relatively unexplored. Mount Paget, the island's highest peak, rises to 9,625 feet and was not ascended until 1965. South Georgia is rugged and treeless, but mosses, lichens, and grasses hug the ground, as if deliberately ducking from the high winds and cold air. The vegetation nourishes reindeer, brought to the island almost a hundred years ago.

The surrounding Antarctic sea is brimming with life. Phytoplankton, the lowest link in the Antarctic marine food chain, thrive in these waters, supporting krill, squid, fish, and whales. The island draws many summer residents: Birds

nest in the ice-free regions. Plumed-headed macaroni penguins and large colonies of mighty elephant seals and Antarctic fur seals swim here to breed. So while South Georgia's remote location may look accidental, it is important for a variety of Antarctic creatures.

The great Antarctic explorer Ernest Shackleton is buried on South Georgia Island. He died while on his last exploration, and his grave is a symbol of the longing that drew him back to the hostile but beautiful landscapes of the polar regions.

Greenland

Denmark When Viking explorer Eric the Red returned to Iceland from this huge island in A.D. 985, he named it Greenland to encourage his people to come here to colonize. In fact, there is not much green about Greenland: About 85 percent of the island is covered in a thick, permanent ice sheet. There are some trees in the south, but not enough for a forest. Brimming with marine wildlife, sparsely populated—just seven people per hun-dred square miles—and largely pollution-free, Greenland is a true wilderness. But as if it were not wild enough on its own, a huge chunk of eastern Greenland—25 percent of the island's area—is designated as North East Greenland National Park. The park, largest in the world, protects all mammals, birds, plants, and archaeological sites.

Established as a wilderness reserve, the park, which lies wholly above the Arctic Circle, is now open to resourceful tourists, but remains primarily a sanctuary for arctic wildlife. Its myriad fjords provide habitat and respite for whales, walruses, and seals, tired of the tough life of the high seas. The park's tundra offers nesting grounds for several species of birds. Greenland's polar bears find their most important breeding grounds in the park. And one of the world's last wild herds of musk oxen makes its home in the park. Greenland, more environmentally intact than most parts of the world, may not be green in color but is in spirit.

Franz Josef Land

Russia Huge icebergs float freely in the Arctic Ocean around the 191-island Franz Josef Land Archipelago. The 6,229-square-mile archipelago is as far north as one can go in Russia; the islands are closer to the North Pole than to the Arctic Circle. Even in summer, average temperatures barely climb over 35°F.

Not surprisingly, few creatures can thrive here. On land, the arctic fox hunts birds, its long fur fluffing in the wind. Off the coast, half-ton polar bears jump from floe to floe, and thick-skinned seals and ivory-tusked walruses swim the chilly waters. Many bird species nest on the islands of the archipelago.

The islands are mainly plateaus, and up to 85 percent of them are buried in ice. The ice-free areas support some plants: rock-hugging lichens and mosses, and fewer than 40 species of arctic wild-flowers. The Russians send their hardiest citizens to work at their permanent weather stations in Franz Josef Land, but though the tours of duty are relatively short, for human beings here all time runs long.

ARCTIC OCEAN

GREENLAND
(DENMARK)

ALASKA
(U.S.)

Yukon

*Mt. McKinley
(Denali)
20,320 ft
6,194 m*

Denali
N.P. &
Preserve

Wrangell-
St. Elias N.P.
and
Preserve

*Mt. Logan
19,551 ft
5,959 m*

Kluane
National
Park
Reserve

Mackenzie

*Great
Bear Lake*

Nahanni
National
Park
Reserve

*Great
Slave Lake*

*Hudson
Bay*

L'Eau
Claire
Wilderness

Peace

Nelson

Saskatchewan

C A N A D A

Olympic
Peninsula

Olympic
National Park

Columbia

Sawtooth
N.R.A.

Yellowstone

*Lake
Winnipeg*

*Great
Lakes*

St. Lawrence

Baxter
State
Park

PACIFIC

OCEAN

Sawtooth
Wilderness

Yellowstone N.P.

Grand
Teton
N.P.

Badlands

Mississippi

Missouri

U N I T E D   S T A T E S

Colorado

Ohio

Great
Dismal
Swamp

ATLANTIC

OCEAN

Mazatzal
Wilderness

Big Bend
Ranch
S.P.

Black Gap
Wildlife
Management
Area

Mississippi

Okefenokee
Swamp

*Sonoran
Desert*

*Chihuahuan
Desert*

Rio Grande

*Baja
California*

Gulf of California

Big Bend
National
Park

*Mississippi
Delta*

BAHAMAS

*Gulf of
Mexico*

DOMINICAN
REPUBLIC

MEXICO

*Lacandón
Wilderness*

CUBA

PUERTO
RICO
(U.S.)

BELIZE

HAITI

JAMAICA

Caribbean   Sea

GUATEMALA

HONDURAS

NICARAGUA

EL SALVADOR

COSTA RICA

PANAMA

La Amistad
Biosphere
Reserve

0   400 Mi

0   600 Km

North America

by Noel Grove

On no other continent has so much wilderness disappeared so rapidly as in North America. On the other hand, this is the continent where the idea of preserving natural areas took root.

To Europeans, whose cities were teeming and whose open spaces were claimed, North America was an unspoiled land of opportunity. The more they examined it, the more diverse it appeared, with forests, wetlands, vast plains, and formidable mountains. The prevailing view toward this new land was expressed by young merchant Josiah Gregg as he rode down the Santa Fe Trail in 1831: "All who have traversed these delightful regions look forward to the day when the Indian title to the land shall be extinguished and flourishing white settlements dispel the gloom which at present prevails over this uninhabited region."

The dramatic alteration of the New World began with the first permanent European colonists in the 16th century. Within 300 years their descendants had looked into most corners of that enormous area and changed much of it. The extent of change became apparent through the decline of creatures that once thrived here. Wolves were reduced to a handful. Millions of bison shrank to only a few hundred. The passenger pigeon all but disappeared. By 1870, some in the New World were wondering how to save what was left. Gregg's gloom over too much wildness had been replaced by concern that too little remained.

Alarm over vanishing wilderness resulted in the first national parks, and the first legislation designating wilderness areas where nature, not man, prevails. Today, tracts of swamp, forest, desert, and mountain remain that would look familiar to the eagle, the wolf, or the bear of four centuries ago. Islands of the past, they remind us of the world that once existed here, and of beauty worth saving.

Last stand of the Ice Age can be seen in summer melting of Alsek Glacier in the St. Elias Mountains. Nearly 30 thousand square miles in the Wrangells and St. Elias of Alaska and the Yukon Territory represent some of the continent's last great wilderness areas, where wild beauty is protected as parkland.

Kluane and Wrangell–St. Elias

The Wrangell and St. Elias mountain ranges were pushed into safekeeping. The process began millions of years ago when a piece of earth's crust in the Pacific Ocean crashed into North America. That monumental collision formed the two mountain ranges. The resulting spires presented barricades to human intrusion that left land unchanged for centuries, an enclave that one early explorer referred to as "God-given mighty wilderness of majesty, freedom, and peace...."

Most of it remains that way. The border between the United States and Canada cuts through these mountains, and the two nations now protect more than 18.6 million acres back to back, an area larger than New Hampshire, Vermont, and Massachusetts combined. In Alaska, the Wrangell-St. Elias National Park and Preserve is the United State's largest park, almost six times bigger than Yellowstone. Kluane National Park Reserve in the Yukon Territory is one of the largest and wildest of Canada's parklands.

They are parks in name only. From a high peak you can turn in all directions and see no evidence that people inhabit this planet. Kluane lists 13 trails but only one campground, and Congress has directed the U.S. Park Service to maintain the mountains, valleys, streams, and lakes of Wrangell-St. Elias "in their natural state."

The natural state on both sides of the border is the Great Outdoors, constructed on enormous scale. Three of the volcanic Wrangells reach above 16,000 feet. Piercing clouds just miles from the Pacific, the St. Elias is the highest mountain range in North America and has some of the tallest coastal mountains in the world. It includes Mount Logan, highest peak in Canada at 19,545 feet. At 18,008, Mount St. Elias is second in the U.S. only to Mount McKinley. Five other peaks top 15,000 feet.

The largest collection of glaciers outside the polar regions slides off the shoulders of these giants. In size and profusion they offer a glimpse of the last ice age and are, in fact, leftovers from that time. More than 150 separate glaciers creep down the valleys of Wrangell-St. Elias Park and Preserve, and one of them, Malaspina, is larger than Rhode Island. Ice fields cover more than two-thirds of Kluane. Where the ice stops, meandering rivers braid the rugged landscape.

Summer is a brief visitor, but this is no lifeless deep freeze. Dall sheep browse in alpine meadows, and caribou occupy the tundra. Both are preyed upon by wolves and grizzly bears. Salmon spawn in the streams, and trout thrive in lakes of snowmelt, overflown by numerous migratory birds. Moose munch greenery in the wetlands, and, on the U.S. side, bison graze on riverbanks. Numerous smaller creatures feed lynx, wolverines, otters, and bald eagles.

Despite the rigors of climate and cliff, game drew people, and

remnants of humanity date back 8,000 years. Modern sounds did not invade until the dawn of this century, when attempts were made to exploit minerals. From 1911 to 1938 a railroad carved into the hillsides on the U.S. side hauled out billions of dollars' worth of copper. In Canada, dreams of gold brought outsiders to the mountains, and while nuggets were found, riches were not.

Kluane miners left little but horse trails and graveyards.

Today, a rough gravel road reaches within a mile of the little town of McCarthy and the nearby remnants of the Kennicott copper mine. Visitors must cross a surging river by swaying hand tram to reach McCarthy's scattering of houses, one old hotel, and bar with batwing doors. At the top of the huge park another gravel road arcs 46 miles into the Wrangells and stops at a home of hunting guides. Beyond both roads lie hundreds of miles of profound wilderness. Kluane's rough roads total less than 30 miles, and the longest penetrates the park only 14 miles.

The scattering of hikers, big-game hunters, and mountain climbers is virtually unnoticeable in the enormousness. For all the modern tools of outdoorsmanship, every year lives are lost in the cold, rushing streams, in falls by ice climbers, in the myriad ways that raw nature can ambush fragile flesh.

The grandeur of both parks is viewed largely from the air as bush pilots contract their services to sightseers. Plane rides can be expensive, though, and in the U.S. park there is some public pressure to improve access into the parklands, create campsites, and develop trails.

The primitive quality of the Kluane and Wrangell-St. Elias ranges continues, however, a monument to post-Ice Age purity and a challenge to those who would dare to enter some of the most rugged, untouched terrain in the world.

Barriers of rock and cold long kept development from far north ranges such as Kluane (opposite). Until dreams of mineral wealth drove humanity to such forbidding terrain early in the 20th century, it remained a sanctuary of the grizzly bear (below) and the bald eagle (above). Although restricted hunting is now allowed, the few roads and trails help preserve the region as a wildlife domain.

Mountains in a deep freeze, peaks of the St. Elias rise above the largest ice fields outside the polar regions. Moist winds sweeping off the Pacific bring precipitation that can fall as snow any month of the year on the continent's highest coastal range. Glaciers inching off slopes pool in the valleys.

God's Great Plough

Just as your hands can press fluffy snow into a heavy ball, continually accumulating snowfall compresses the snow beneath it into solid ice, and gravity creates a slow-flowing glacier. Today's mountain glaciers, born at elevations where more snow accumulates in the winter than can be melted in the summer, are pale imitations of the massive ice sheets that blanketed a third of the planet during ice ages. Formed at high latitudes, they build to such thicknesses that the tremendous weight forces them to spread. Mountain glacier or continental sheet, these rivers of ice grind rock into powder, gouge valleys, and move boulders, reshaping the land and causing an early glaciologist to refer to them as "God's great plough."

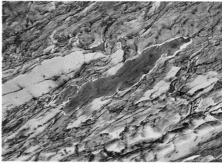

Through fog of their own making in the sharp fall air, elk move across a meadow in Yellowstone. Herds have so thrived that wolves were reintroduced to control their numbers. Although the famous park includes two million acres, surrounding wildlands create a complete ecosystem seven times that size.

Yellowstone

In mountainous country thick with forest that borders Wyoming, Montana, and Idaho, an idea caught fire more than a century ago that has spread around the globe. The area known as Yellowstone became the world's first national park in 1872, set aside so a whole nation could experience lavish scenery, marvel at natural wonders fed by volcanism, and observe wildlife wandering free.

Each year more than three million people enter the gates of this 2.2-million-acre park, the largest national park in the contiguous 48 states. Yellowstone has become a testing ground for natural ecosystems beset by public pressure. Its founders could not have imagined the volumes of people that would someday flock here, but one of its early explorers was prophetic when he called the area "probably the greatest laboratory that nature furnishes on the surface of the globe."

If laboratories bring chemistry to mind, there is plenty of that. Magmatic heat from a hot spot burst through the crust of the earth here 600,000 years ago in a series of gigantic explosions that scattered ash as far away as present-day Mississippi. The geothermal cauldron beneath the park continues to feed 60 percent of the world's geysers, at least two of them spuming 250 feet into the air. Bacteria create springs colored red, yellow, green, orange, and brown. The volcano's persistent violence can be witnessed at one cliff where 27 layers of fossilized forests are visible lying one atop the other, buried in successive eruptions over centuries.

Catastrophic though they may be, volcanoes leave fertile soils scattered in their wakes, and the recovered vegetation draws legions of wildlife. Native Americans were drawn to Yellowstone in its pre-park days by abundant herds of elk, bison, mule deer, bighorn sheep, moose, and pronghorn. Beavers plied the creeks, and grizzly and black bears roamed the shores. Wolves and mountain lions kept the grazers in population balance.

Today, groves of lodgepole pine, Douglas fir, Engelmann spruce, and quaking aspen cover four-fifths of Yellowstone in forest. In summer, wildflowers adorn meadows rimmed by high mountains. Snowmelt from them feeds huge Yellowstone Lake, which covers 136 square miles, and at an elevation of 7,733 feet, North America's largest alpine lake. Many smaller lakes dot the park. Yellowstone River, largest of several river systems, has carved a jagged gorge known as the Grand Canyon of the Yellowstone. Until it joins the Missouri after flowing 671 miles, it remains the longest free-running river in the United States with no dams or controls.

Numerous smaller streams drain the highlands, flowing both east and west off the Continental Divide and prompting mountain man Jim Bridger to report that a trout could choose to swim to either the Atlantic or the Pacific. A renowned yarn-spinner, Bridger was not believed when he first returned from Yellowstone and told of "a mountain of transparent glass," now known as Obsidian Cliff, and pools of water that were "boiling hot." When most of his tales were finally verified, Congress set aside the wonderland for all to see.

Today 370 miles of paved roads lead to 12 campgrounds and, within park boundaries, 9 lodges and hotels. Yellowstone in summer sometimes resembles a small city, where traffic jams and accidents are common. Campgrounds experience vandalism and robberies. About 1,200 miles of trails lace the backcountry.

Not respectful of boundaries, the large animals range far beyond the park, over a more extensive wild area known as the Greater Yellowstone ecosystem. The combination of public and private lands totals some 18 million acres, one of the largest conglomerations of wildlands remaining in the United States. To the south is Grand Teton National Park, and in the three states touching Yellowstone Park are Forest Service wilderness areas. Bureau of Land Management holdings, non-wilderness national forests, three national wildlife refuges, and state and private lands complete the mosaic. In some public areas multiple-use activities

Water wonders have drawn visitors to Yellowstone for more than a century. Geothermal heat fuels Castle Geyser (above) and many other steamy spectaculars. The deep canyon carved by the Yellowstone River includes 308-foot Lower Falls, (opposite).

such as livestock grazing, timber cutting, and mineral extraction are allowed. The lands exempt from such activities total about six million acres, but they are islands affected by the activity around them.

Yellowstone park is still home to some 30,000 elk, one of the largest herds in the world, and some of the last herds of free-ranging bison. Some 250 grizzlies roam the wilds of the park and adjacent areas, the last large sanctuary for them outside Alaska. Trumpeter swans, nearly wiped out by pioneers who shot these low-flying giants, live here year-round. Bald eagles and ospreys soar above the cliffs and tall trees. With the return of wolves to the park in 1995, the roll call of wildlife species remains much the same as it was two centuries ago.

Economic activity in adjacent lands raises the biggest concerns for

Yellowstone

Is It Still Wild?

With three million visitors a year, traffic jams, and urban crime, our most celebrated national park sounds like a giant parking lot, but park officials point out that only two percent of Yellowstone is developed. Trails crisscross the backcountry, but the numbers of overnight hikers are limited by a permit system. At peak season in July and August, an average of 30,000 people a day may be wandering through a mostly forested area larger than Delaware and Rhode Island combined. Animals speak best for the wildness of Yellowstone, for thousands of creatures suspicious of human presence make their home here. "The ones you see from the road have traditionally used that area, and grown tolerant of human presence," said ranger Anita Varley, backcountry supervisor. "If you encounter an elk, deer, or bear in the backcountry, you're probably not going to see it very long."

Yellowstone

At home on the range, bison graze in verdant Hayden Valley. Before its discovery by white explorers, the Yellowstone region was frequently visited by Native Americans seeking its ample herds of wildlife. Today, bison frequently injure tourists who mistake their calm appearance for tameness.

Yellowstone National Park. Mining activities could affect the water. Oil and gas developers want to lease multiple-use public lands for exploration, which means building roads that unzip more wilderness to human traffic. On private lands, added vacation homes create more roads and human presence. Logging clouds streams and affects animal habitat. "In one area of bear management, 70 percent of the vegetation was removed either by logging or fire," says Robert Ekey of the watchdog group Greater Yellowstone Coalition in Bozeman, Montana.

Activity within the park has increased in winter as snowmobiling on

unplowed roads has become a popular sport. On a busy weekend about 1,400 snowmobiles churn from the west gate to Old Faithful, their snarling two-cycle engines leaving a blue haze in the valleys and disrupting the solitude of cross-country skiers. The Park Service is considering a reservation system that would limit their numbers. Remedies for summer traffic might include mass transit systems, but as one park representative said, "There's no money for that right now."

Attempts at over-managing the park in the past were not satisfactory. A predator-control program that removed the wolf and decimated the cougar population allowed elk herds to grow until some believe the habitat could not support them. Some scientists believe suppression of the forest fires that were once part of the cycles of Yellowstone forests allowed large amounts of combustible tinder to accumulate. An extremely dry summer in 1988 resulted in a wide-ranging conflagration unpopular with the general public, but not permanently damaging to the park.

Although more natural management is now favored, a policy of "letting nature take its course" is probably no longer adequate because of human influences in or near the park. For all the tourism it supports, the Greater Yellowstone area offers a testing ground for policies and methods that accommodate both nature and human impacts. If it can now lead a nation toward protection of other beleaguered wild and natural areas, its contributions as a laboratory will match its beauty as a wonderland.

A Predator Returns

The howl of the wolf echoes through Yellowstone again. Earlier this century when *Canis lupus* was shot, trapped, and poisoned as official government policy, wolves were considered vermin. Studies since then have revealed that they cull weaker animals, thereby improving the genetic stock, and do not wipe our their prey completely. In the 1990s the same government that had removed them authorized their return, despite objections from ranchers that wolves would endanger their livestock. Fourteen wolves were released in the park in 1995, and 17 more were released in 1996. By early 1996, nine pups had been born and nine wolves had died. One wolf was shot by government hunters after it killed several sheep. The owner was compensated from a fund set up by the environmental group Defenders of Wildlife.

Water of two minds, Yellowstone Lake has cold glacial melt at the surface and boiling spots at geothermal outlets on the bottom (left).

Warm waters offer a midwinter spa for trumpeter swans (opposite), which arrive from Canada.

Long-lived but late to flower, the broad-leaved agave plant may wait two decades before displaying its only blossom. Another late-bloomer, Big Bend in Texas was long seen as a wasteland until it became a national park. Three vegetation zones offer scenes from stark desert to high woodland.

Big Bend

*A*fter traveling south for nearly a thousand miles, the Rio Grande, which divides Texas and Mexico, suddenly turns back toward the northeast, creating an arc known as the Big Bend. It cradles a desert of deep-cut canyons, basaltic mountains, and arid plains of cactus and creosote bush. The first Spanish explorers called it *despoblado,* "the uninhabited place," but Big Bend contains a surprising variety of plants and wildlife. At the tip of the arc is a 1,250-square-mile national park that was created in 1944.

Big Bend draws people who prefer their outdoor experiences without crowds, for it is one of the least-visited national parks in the United States. "Our visitors don't just stop by here, they make this a destination," said Valerie Naylor at park headquarters. "We're 126 miles from the nearest inter-state, 225 miles from the nearest sizable airport." When people arrive, they're usually equipped to get out of their cars and see the park close-up.

For all its appearance of wasteland, it's a land accustomed to change. Now part of the vast Chihuahuan Desert that extends into Mexico, limestone sediments indicate the Big Bend area was covered by an ocean some 200 million years ago. Now-silent volcanoes built the Chisos Mountains, the most southerly range in the continental United States, and left chimneys of igneous rock in the desert. When the seas were replaced by low-lying swamps, dinosaurs wandered where today a rattlesnake would dry up in the midday heat.

Pre-park people living here were as tough as the scrub brush that clings to life. Fierce Mescalero Apaches, who knew every water source, every hiding place in the rocks, made this a last Native American stronghold. Comanches raided Mexico through Big Bend country so often that their horses and stolen cattle left a trail visible for decades. With the Indians finally overwhelmed by U.S. and Mexican troops around 1880, ranchers moved in. They left when overgrazing wiped out the few green enclaves that nature had built over millennia. Recovery is now under way.

More than 40 species of cactuses grow here, more than in any other national park. Most common is the prickly pear, food for animals and people able to avoid its needles. The eagle's claw and fishhook cactuses have spines too painful to penetrate and so thick they shade the stem from the sun.

Where Apaches once dwelled, claret cups blossom in the Chisos Mountains. The last stand of the fierce fighters came in these volcanic structures, eroded into twisting canyons that offered numerous places to hide. Pines and firs usually seen in moist climates testify to Big Bend's twisted past; dinosaurs roamed long-ago swamps, and 12,000 years ago heavy rains fell on today's desert.

Other plants have developed protection against aridity. The thorny ocotillo cuts down on water needs by dropping its leaves completely in drought. Its tall stems look dead, protruding like clusters of buggy whips, but with the spring rains they bloom with new leaves. The *lechuguilla,* found only in the Chihuahuan Desert, grows spiked, purple foliage, but its moisture-laden parts are underground. When it blooms after a decade or so, an asparagus-

like stalk shoots as high as 15 feet into the air. Javelinas, or wild pigs, dig up the moist roots, and mule deer munch on the bloomstalk.

Animals find many ways to cope with the heat and dryness. Huge, veined ears on the black-tailed jackrabbit dissipate heat. The roadrunner rarely drinks, but derives moisture from prey such as lizards and small snakes. The dark-ling beetle has an air space under its wings as insulation against the heat. Most of the 70-plus species of mammals move about in the cool of night.

Desert bighorn sheep dis-appeared around the turn of the century, but a few pronghorn remain, as does a subspecies of deer called the Sierra del Carmen whitetail, found only in the United States in the Chisos. Mountain lions ambush them, but another predator, the Mexican wolf, was wiped out decades ago, as was the Mexican black bear. The bear has returned on its own, crossing the Rio Grande from the south.

An unwelcome new species being eradicated is the tamarisk tree, brought by settlers as a wind-break. It uses valuable water at a high rate and is inedible for ani-mals and useless to man. Another environmental problem is air pol-lution from a Mexican coal-fired power plant that spreads a haze over once-clear desert air.

Fog pools in Juniper Canyon, cooling the feet of the Chisos, the only range entirely within a U.S. national park. Summer brings moisture from the Gulf of Mexico, but winters are dry and surprisingly cold in the high-lands. The extremes of rainfall and temperature, depending on the elevation, result in a wide variety of plants and ani-mals. Some 70 species of mammals live here, but Big Bend is best known for having more than 40 species of cactuses, unmatched by any other park.

Otherwise, Big Bend is well-protected from adjacent human develop-ments, with Big Bend Ranch State Park to the west and the state-owned Black Gap Wildlife Management Area to the east. Heat and hardship should long insure its wildness, but for those who find beauty in the play of sun on stone and the special adaptation of plants and animals in the park, Big Bend will remain a special place to visit.

Olympic

Automobiles were being built and Seattle and Tacoma were growing when the last corner of wilderness in the lower United States was still largely unknown. On a clear day, citizens of the two young cities could look across Puget Sound at the mysterious Olympic Peninsula and its snow-covered mountains. An area larger than several Eastern states remained a 6,500-square-mile blank on the North American map. As late as 1889, Washington's governor-elect Elisha Ferry called it the state's great unknown land, "like the interior of Africa." It was whispered darkly that cannibals lurked among those trackless peaks.

This quadrangular chunk of land had remained secret while the remainder of a young, new nation grew comfortable with itself, simply because it was too difficult to enter. The mountains, comprising about half the peninsula, rose abruptly from near sea level to heights just below 8,000 feet and were slashed with deep canyons cut by angry rivers. Their shoulders were robed in snowfields and glaciers; their rain-swept lower flanks wore virgin forests so dense that light barely penetrated. Until curiosity and the thirst for fame got the better of a few hardy souls, nobody bothered to go there.

Physically, as well as spiritually, the Olympic Peninsula was a land apart. Geologists believe it came from elsewhere, a piece of offshore ridge that buckled when an oceanic plate slid under North America's western coast. Glaciers helped keep it separate from the mainland by carving moats on two sides: the Strait of Juan de Fuca on the north and Puget Sound to the east, as well as the Hood Canal that reaches in from the sound deep into the eastern slopes. These watery barriers left the peninsula out of the migratory paths of many animals normally found at comparable latitudes, such as grizzly bears, wolverines, and bighorn sheep. And they may have isolated a large herbivore that developed on its own, the Roosevelt elk.

For two centuries after a Greek sailor traveling under the Spanish name of Juan de Fuca sailed along the north shore of the peninsula in 1592, the place was ignored by Europeans. Native Americans living in the low-lands killed two of the first parties of Europeans that tried to land, but in 1788 an English captain named John Meares tarried when he struck up a friendship with Indians fishing at the northernmost tip. The highest peak

The mystery surrounding the Olympic Mountains was cleared up little more than a century ago, when adventurers first crossed the Olympic Peninsula. The last corner of the contiguous 48 states to be explored, the region features one of the country's few temperate rain forests.

looked to him like the home of the gods of Greek mythology, and he called it Mount Olympus. Four years later surveyor George Vancouver called the range the Olympic Mountains, and the name eventually stuck to the whole peninsula.

At first only mountain men penetrated the dense forests. The first known crossing from Port Angeles in the north to Grays Harbor in the south took place in the winter of 1889-90 by an expedition sponsored by the Seattle *Press* and led by James Christie. Young Joseph O'Neil, who had led an expedition in 1885, headed more extensive explorations in the summer of 1890. In late 1890, with the first crossing and his own excursions still fresh in American minds, O'Neil suggested that timber would be a valuable resource in parts of the region but the rugged interior might best be designated a national park. He lived to see it happen, in 1938.

Olympic National Park is really three parks in one, with three distinct ecosystems. Behind a narrow length of fog-shrouded, sandy coastline lies one of the few rain forests in the lower 48 states. At higher levels are sub-alpine zones with alternating firs, flowered meadows, sparkling lakes, and active glaciers.

An Eden long isolated by rugged landscape, Olympic Peninsula became a haven for less-known species such as the black-tailed deer (opposite). A herbivore more rare, the Roosevelt elk was named for the outdoor-loving President who first set aside the area to save the unique subspecies. His national monument achieved park status in 1938. Moisture sweeping off the Pacific feeds soaring stands of conifers where light barely sifts through to the spongy forest floor (below).

The peninsula's rain forests—in valleys of the Quinault, Queets, and Hoh Rivers—are some of the few temperate rain forests in the world. Others are in New Zealand, southern Chile, and Japan. Moisture-laden air from the Pacific dumps some 145 inches on the Olympic valleys annually, creating towering cathedrals of Sitka spruce that can be almost 59 feet around and reach heights of 300 feet. Ferns and mosses trail from their limbs; more mosses, lichens, and shrubs carpet the forest floor, and the light that suffuses this abundant vegetation is tinted an eerie green. So thick is the ground cover that many tree seedlings get their start by germinating on rotting logs, then stretch toward the sky in neat rows as the "nurse log" gradually disintegrates. The rampant plant growth is said to be the greatest weight of living matter, per acre, in the world.

As the Pacific air passes over the mountains, even more moisture is condensed by the cooler air so that at least 200 inches a year drops on those ramparts, mostly in the form of snow. The snow compresses into glaciers, and some 60 slide off the Olympic peaks. So much moisture

Some 8,000 feet stretch from pebbled Rialto Beach (below) to the spires of Mount Olympus (opposite), which are visible for more than a hundred miles. Glaciers by the dozen creep down the steep slopes, and although some 600 trails crisscross the park, only the hardiest hikers venture into these high pavilions.

Olympic

Sentinels of solitude, spruce trees line Kalaloch Beach on the 50-mile coastline added to the park in 1953. Such privacy may be short-lived; crowds that impact other national parks are also expected here. Environmentalists regret the loss of wildlife habitat outside the park's boundaries.

is sucked from the clouds that 30 miles from rain forest, the northeastern side of the peninsula gets less than 20 inches of rainfall a year.

Within the park are found rare Roosevelt elk, named for Theodore Roosevelt who created Mount Olympus National Monument to save the unique animals. Larger than their Rocky Mountain cousins, Roosevelt elk also have white rumps and thicker antlers. Unlike elk at Yellowstone, few are seen by the 4.6 million annual visitors to Olympic park because of their extreme shyness, perhaps a result of overhunting once their domain was opened. Deer, black bear, cougar, and numerous smaller mammals share their wild haunts, some 422,000 acres of protected land.

If the parklands remain largely unaffected, the same cannot be said

for the remainder of the peninsula. Nearly half is owned privately, most of that by industrial forest companies. Of the dense, old-growth forests that daunted the early explorers, less than 20 percent remain. Towns, farms, and country homes dot the periphery of the park itself, removing winter habitat for the shy elk and summer forests for other wildlife that once lived there.

Today, Highway 101 touches the north end of the park and spur roads lead into forested lowlands, but the high, wild interior can be reached only by foot on some 600 miles of trails. The secrets of the last mysterious wilderness of the lower 48 states have been laid all too bare, but the grandeur that drew its first explorers can still be seen within the park's boundaries.

Wetlands

We used to consider them wastelands, land too wet to farm, havens for mosquitoes and snakes. The Swamp Wetlands Acts of 1849 gave away 65 million acres of wetlands to 15 states to be reclaimed for levees, canals, or farmlands. It is a measure of our changing attitude toward wetlands that in 1970 the environmental organization called the Nature Conservancy received a corporate gift of 50,000 acres of the Great Dismal Swamp in Virginia so that the wetland might be preserved.

Far from wastelands, these mucky, often fetid jungles of ooze are hotbeds of life, more lucrative in terms of energy created than a Kansas wheat field. The most productive wetlands can produce 12 tons of biomass per acre per year, far exceeding grasslands and many forests. Microscopic animals feed on algae. These small creatures are eaten in turn by insects that are eaten by small fish, which fall prey to birds, mammals, and larger fish. In warm-climate wetlands, the largest predators may be crocodilians—alligators, caimans in Central and South America, crocodiles, and needle-nosed gavials of India.

Wetlands cover no more than six percent of the earth, but they play important roles. Coastal marshes are nurseries for commercial fish that in adulthood move to the open sea. As of 1985, more than three million people have spent nearly one billion dollars annually in North America hunting waterfowl, and almost six times more found pleasure in observing and photographing birds such as egrets, cranes, loons, and ibises. Water percolating through wetlands helps recharge groundwater. The dense vegetation traps sediments and filters pollutants. By retaining water and releasing it slowly, wetlands are helpful in flood control. Massachusetts saved millions of dollars by preserving marshes along the Charles River rather than building dams.

For all their value, wetlands have been destroyed throughout the world by human development, farming in particular. Of the roughly 220 million acres of wetlands in the contiguous United States when settlers arrived, less than half remain. Canada, which has a large portion of the world's wetlands, has experienced losses in certain regions ranging from 32 to 61 percent.

In 1994 the United States, Canada, and Mexico jointly signed the North American Waterfowl Management Plan, resulting in nearly five million acres being protected or restored. A voluntary Wetlands Reserve program in the United States funds property owners who restore wetlands and is flooded with applicants. Canada has wetland-saving

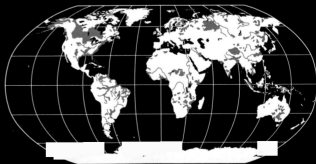

■ Wetlands

initiatives in every province. Similar initiatives are under way in southern Africa and Southeast Asia, and international environmental organizations are expanding wetland conservation activities.

Net losses continue globally, but numerous programs indicate that the destruction may be slowing. As science learns more about the systems by which living plants and animals transfer energy, we finally may be realizing the true value of these soggy but indispensable environments.

An arc of triumph for wetland plenty, pelicans crowd a salt marsh in the Mississippi Delta. Soggy ground was once given away to anyone who would drain it, but today laws protect wetlands for their high productivity. Still, thousands of acres disappear every year.

Okefenokee

Okefenokee Swamp remains wild in the populous southeastern United States because of its own resilience. Efforts to drain it and cut most of its valuable timber began in the 1890s and were thwarted by collapsing canals and mounting expenses. Today one of the the largest freshwater wetlands in the contiguous United States retains the mystery and beauty it has held through the centuries, in 650 square miles of primeval forest with bellowing alligators and moss-draped cypress.

For all its resemblance to the age of dinosaurs, the Okefenokee is not very old. The basin that holds the swamp was formed 250,000 years ago when the Atlantic Ocean reached into what is now Georgia and Florida. The sea created a sandbar about 40 miles off that earlier shore, and when the ocean receded it left a shallow lagoon. The basin gradually lined itself with dead vegetation that decayed into peat, and the swamp achieved its present form less than 8,000 years ago. Continued decomposition releases tannic acids that tint the water a tea-colored brown. The basin is slightly elevated in the north, and its waters flow very slowly southward, feeding the St. Marys and Suwannee Rivers.

The chemistry of decay in the peat named the place. Sometimes buoyant gases, the by-product of anaerobic decay, become trapped under a layer of peat and elevate a large fragment to the surface. Seeds germinate on the floating mat, and growing plants—including small and full-size trees—send down roots that anchor it to the bottom. Native Americans noted that the ground moved when they stepped on these small islands and called them Okefenokee—"trembling earth." At least 70 other islands in the swamp have different geological origins and offer firm footing.

Some 40 species of fish find a home in the dark brew. They include chain pickerel, largemouth bass, and channel catfish, all popular with the sport-fishing crowd. Human visitors should be grateful for a smaller resident, the mosquito fish, which feeds on larvae of the winged tormentors. Drawn to the small aquatic life are large numbers of wading birds such as cranes, herons, egrets, ibises, and spoonbills. Hawks, vultures, and, in winter, an occasional bald eagle circle the skies. Raccoons, otters, black bears, and white-tailed deer tread through the water as well as on solid ground.

Bejeweled by the sun, the monarch of the Okefenokee basks in water tea-colored by decaying vegetation. Despite a marked recovery over three decades, alligators are today listed as threatened. Hundreds still reign in the Okefenokee, adding a chill to the primeval mystery of this unique wetland of the Southeast.

Big feet help bald cypress trees stay erect in the swamp and may also channel oxygen. Long legs aid the sandhill crane, (opposite), one of

many wading birds found here.

PAGES 222-223
An echo of the Carboniferous. Okefenokee steams in a low sun.

King of the swamp has always been the American alligator, which can grow up to 15 feet long and weigh 500 pounds, and feeds mostly on snakes, fish, turtles, and small mammals.

Burial mounds and remnants of pottery point to human presence in Okefenokee as early as 2000 B.C. Seminole Indians later used it as a base for raiding white settlers until they were driven out by the U.S. Army in

Okefenokee

the 1850s. Long before the cutting of timber had stopped, a call arose for preserving the swamp. Francis Harper, one of several scientists researching Okefenokee, wrote after a visit in 1912, "Its majestic pines and cypresses, its peaceful waterways, and lily strewn prairies, together with the splendid wild creatures

that inhabit them, should be safeguarded from destruction."

In 1937 about half of Okefenokee became a national wildlife refuge. Now boaters can rent canoes for sojourns through the 396,000-acre refuge. Quiet paddlers

can pass within yards of large alligators sunning on logs. Five species of poisonous snakes live in the refuge, but no visitor who stayed on established foot paths has ever been bitten. Firefighters and refuge workers who leave well-used areas have been less fortunate, but no deaths have been recorded.

Although the area within the refuge is safe from commercial development, a proposal for mining the metals zircon, staurolite, and titanium from private lands nearby has raised concerns. Mining operations would extend along most of the eastern border, possibly affecting the quality of air and water entering the refuge. "If you alter the way water runs into the swamp, the damage might be irreversible," said refuge manager Mallory Reeves.

Even well-intentioned alterations made years ago are now under suspicion, Reeves added. A dam built where the Okefenokee meets the Suwannee to regulate water levels may be preventing the periodic wildfires that keep Okefenokee from filling in with vegetation. A study is now under way to determine whether the dam should be dismantled and the swamp allowed to regulate itself, as it has done quite nicely for several thousand years.

When Plants Bite Back

When plants need nitrogen that is missing from boggy, acidic soils, they sometimes acquire it from the bodies of animals they catch and consume. Best known is the Venus's flytrap of North and South Carolina, whose open, oval leaves quickly close on insects that touch more than one hair. Enzymes digest the insects within two weeks. Aquatic bladderworts of North America and elsewhere actually suck in food. Underwater, a bulbous part of the stem has air inside a closed flap. When prey touches sensitive hairs near the flap, it swings open long enough for water to rush inside, carrying a water flea or mosquito larvae with it. Pitcher plants, found globally, have leaves shaped like hollow containers with fluid at the bottom. Insects slide down the slippery sides and drown in the fluid, where they are digested. Large ones in Borneo and Malaysia consume birds and small mammals.

Baja

The first Europeans to land on the 800-mile peninsula now known as Baja California were looking for an island of pearls. Instead, the Spanish explorers found desert, volcanoes, and often death at the hands of fierce Native Americans who had their own ideas about the value of their land. With only a few pearls apparent and little water to sustain a search for them, Mexico's desolate Baja was overlooked for centuries. Today, it is cherished in an increasingly crowded world for a different kind of wealth— its very emptiness.

The parched climate is both the curse that challenges life here and the blessing that so far has prevented congestion. The central desert receives only one to three inches of rainfall a year. Northern and southern extremities get more, so most of the 1.6-million residents of Baja live in the large cities of Tijuana, Ensenada, and Mexicali near the United States border, or in the southern capital of La Paz.

In between, for hundreds of miles, the land appears so barren that it is often described as a moonscape. Desert tinged with cactus and scrub brush is crowned by a ridge of mountains that runs almost the entire length of the peninsula. Volcanic peaks and cinder cones rise abruptly out of the sand. The peninsula is part of the Pacific plate that is sliding toward Alaska. This northward trek tore a strip of land 25 to 150 miles wide from the Mexican mainland, opening the watery gap called the Mar de Cortés by Mexicans and the Gulf of California by Americans, and creating Baja California.

Though it may appear desolate and lifeless, Baja supports some tenacious wildlife. Cholla, creosote bushes, and mesquite go dormant in drought until revived by rain. A tree called the boojum extends wildly curving branches like some thorny, half-buried squid, while the sturdy cardon, one of the world's tallest cactuses, sometimes stretches 50 feet high as if reaching for rain. On the baked ground live several species of rattlesnakes including one without rattles, black-tailed jackrabbits, coyotes, ground squirrels, and lizards, creatures of the hot and thorny world. Through scrub brush flit flycatchers and gnatcatchers, roadrunners, scrub jays and shrikes. The pine and small oaks at higher elevations harbor doves, quail, acorn woodpeckers, and eagles.

The richest life occurs in the gulf, where nutrient upswellings from

As though appealing for moisture, fingers of a cardon cactus reach to the morning sky in the peninsula known as Baja California. This is one of the world's tallest cactuses and also one of many unusual plants and animals finely tuned to life in this sun-baked arm of Mexico, treasured by those who value immensities of silence.

A saddle of granite carved by the wind rides out the vagaries of climate in northern Baja's Cataviña Desert. Here temperatures may rise well over 100°F by day, and winds off nearby seawater can blow in a night chill. From one to three inches of rain fall in the central desert annually, about the same as in Death Valley. Small towns bloom where springs feed rare oases, but most of the Baja's 1.6 million people live in cities at the U.S. border or in far south La Paz. A paved road finished in 1973 opened the area to tourism.

deep canyons attract marine life. More than 800 species of fish and 2,000 species of invertebrates have been counted. Smaller prey draw predators such as marlin, snapper, and yellowfin tuna. "It's a giant fish trap," says 86-year-old Bill Gibbs, a private-plane pilot from San Diego, California, who has flown over Baja for more than half a century. The cornucopia also attracts dolphins and sea lions, and tumults of seabirds that whitewash some 70 islands with guano. In winter the warm waters of the gulf and the lagoons on the Pacific side draw whales—fin, blue, gray, humpback, and sperm.

The marine plenty has also brought people. Sport fishermen came for the marlin and swordfish, and the income bolstered local economies. Then large commercial fleets moved in; by the late 1980s, 40 percent of Mexico's fish production came from the Mar de Cortés. Swarms of sardines that once darkened the sea surface began shrinking, as did the numbers of gulls, boobies, terns, and pelicans that lived off them. Foreign ships stole into the gulf illegally, depleting fish stocks even more. Ashore, irrigation for farming has lowered underground water supplies.

The first top-to-bottom paved road unzipped the peninsula in 1973 and bared it to development. Now vacation homes increasingly dot the water's edge, and hotels have appeared up and down the coast. Once only bush pilots flew to a landing strip at the oasis called Mulegé, stepping out of their planes and into the courtyard of the Hotel Serenidad. With the road's arrival, a retirement community of northerners has grown along the freshwater Rio Mulegé, and satellite television dishes sprout among the date palms. "It's the perfect spot," said a white-haired Californian, cruising a seashell street on her fat-tired bicycle. "No noise, great weather, clean air, fish to eat."

Continuation of those delights depends on careful development and the cautious harvest of marine resources, neither of which is much observed. "Because of Mexico's economic problems there is no money for the equipment and personnel necessary for enforcement of regulations," says Enrique Hambleton of La Paz, a member of the environmental organization Pronatura.

"Land is being bought by development interests at prices small farmers cannot resist," he adds. "Fishing violations are rampant. It's a pretty grim picture. The ruggedness that has long protected the peninsula will filter development somewhat, but there are no guarantees."

Sun-dried but sassy, an elephant seal bellows on the beach. Nutrients in Mar de Cortés , dividing Baja from mainland Mexico, draw rich marine life. Former freshwater source dried by irrigation, the Colorado River delta (below) gleams with brine backed up by high tides.

FOLLOWING PAGES: Living off moist pulp, an elephant tree spreads portly limbs in arid Baja.

Other Wild Places

L'Eau Claire Wilderness

Quebec Protected by hordes of insects in summer and by harsh winter weather, the L' Eau Claire—clear water—Wilderness in northern Quebec has remained a wild sanctuary untouched by civilization. From Lac, or Lake, L'Eau Claire, 750 miles north of Ottawa, west to the Hudson Bay, it is a land riddled with numerous small lakes and streams.

The nearest road is 150 miles south of the lake. Valleys shelter forests of spruce, tamarack, and occasional alder thickets. Caribou moss covers some open ground with a light pastel green, and streams and marshes are lined with sedges and horsetails. Cree Indians and Inuit in the Hudson Bay area hunt caribou in the wilderness as they have for centuries. Visitors are few. The wilderness touches both boreal forest and tundra and is visited by great herds of caribou mainly in the winter. Golden eagles and ospreys soar high above. The partly navigable rivers include numerous whitewater rapids, and portages around waterfalls are often steep, rocky, and through dense brush. Nevertheless, the views of trackless conifer forests, craggy outcrops, and unspoiled waters are spectacular.

Nahanni National Park Reserve

Northwest Territories Those who thirst for a look at North America before human influence might wish to visit this pristine park, 1,840 square miles of wilderness 90 miles from the nearest road. Visitors are limited by the Canadian government to 1,800 annually, but perhaps 800 make the trip.

Nearly twice the height of Niagara Falls, Virginia Falls is the most spectacular undeveloped cataract in Canada. But the most impressive feature of the park is its wildness. In forests of spruce, balsam poplar, and quaking aspen can be seen moose, black bear, beaver, and woodland caribou, and Dall sheep can be found on slopes high above the canyons cut by the river.

Baxter State Park

Maine When the late Maine Governor Percival P. Baxter left more than 200,000 acres of prime eastern woodlands to his state, he wanted the area to remain "forever … in its natural wild state." The park has proved so popular that officials must now limit the number of parking spaces at certain sites to assure that the governor's dream remains a reality. Still, Baxter park is not exactly on the main highways of the East, and its remote location in central Maine has discouraged the crowds seen in other more accessible parks. Some 83,000 people visited the park in 1995, and most of them stay around Mount Katahdin, the highest peak in Maine at 5,267 feet and the northern terminus of the Appalachian Trail.

The Katahdin area is only part of the wilderness experience that visitors can savor. The park includes 46 mountains, several ponds and lakes, numerous waterfalls, and streams filled with trout. Moose, bear, deer, and pine marten live in the northern woods. Loons and coyotes serenade at evening. Deep in the woods, pockets of old-growth trees tower above the forest floor, samplings of the wild experience that Governor Baxter had in mind.

Denali National Park and Preserve

Alaska Hundreds of thousands of people visit Alaska's most popular park every year, but plenty of wild, untrammeled land awaits the more intrepid who don't mind leaving tour buses and trails behind. The park sprawls over six million acres, larger than Massachusetts, and has never been settled. Its crowning glory is Mount McKinley, North America's highest peak at 20,320 feet. The glaciers flowing down its base feed numerous rivers that meander through the park. The mountain looms over treeless tundra and partially wooded taiga. On the tundra grow tussocks of sedges and cotton grass and the occasional dwarf shrubs. In the brief summer they burst into glorious color from blossoms. In the taiga, mostly in river valleys, grow spruce, quaking aspen, alder, balsam poplar, and white birch. The most awesome wild denizen is the grizzly bear, but a healthy male moose or cow with calf will stand one off. Wolves range through the park, preying on moose and caribou calves, and Dall sheep. Large populations of migrating birds visit here in summer to feast on plentiful mosquitoes, which in turn feed on unprotected visitors.

Mazatzal Wilderness

Arizona For those who seek a real wilderness challenge, the rugged Sonoran Desert topped by the Mazatzal Mountains should provide an adequate test. Summer desert temperatures hang above 100°F for weeks at a time. Water holes may be a day's horseback ride apart, and forest rangers recommend that hikers bring their own water. The most characteristic plant in the desert is the saguaro cactus, the statuesque, bent-armed variety that can grow 50 feet tall. In the more temperate climate of the mountains grow forests of ponderosa pine and Douglas fir, the latter a northern species stranded here when the last Ice Age retreated.

Cougars in the mountains prey on mule deer, and coyotes and black bears round out the large predators. Smaller animals include javelinas, skunks, raccoons, and numerous rodents. The saguaro cactuses serve as apartment houses for a number of winged species, including gila woodpeckers, gilded flickers, screech owls, elf owls, kestrels, and cactus wrens.

Sawtooth Wilderness

Idaho These jagged mountains, named for their resemblance to the sharp teeth of a crosscut saw, offer something for both the automotive sightseer and the

MOOSE WADING IN WONDER LAKE, DENALI NATIONAL PARK, ALASKA

known for taking its preservation programs seriously, where some 25 percent of the land is protected. Costa Rica's La Amistad includes more than 2,300 square miles of lowland tropical rain forest, subalpine paramo forest, oak stands, high altitude bogs, and cloud forest. Mammal species within these varied habitats include tapirs, squirrel monkeys, pumas, ocelots, and jaguars. The 400 species of birds identified include nine of Costa Rica's endangered fowl, such as harpy eagles and quetzals. Environmentalists and government officials are optimistic about continued protection of La Armistad because of buffering around it from several Indian reservations, a national park, and a number of other protected areas.

hard-core hiker. The eastern two-thirds of the Sawtooth National Recreation Area is laced with decent roads, both paved and gravel, for the car-bound to admire glorious views from every direction and to drive to four of the largest lakes. That still leaves 217,000 acres of the wild mountain country designated as the Sawtooth Wilderness, where only hikers and horseback riders can venture. Their rewards are flower-strewn mountain meadows and more than 300 alpine lakes of astonishing clarity, some stocked with trout. Rising in all directions are peaks of not only the Sawtooths but also the White Cloud and Boulder ranges, with more than 40 peaks rising 10,000 feet or higher. Large animals include deer, elk, black bear, and coyote, with mountain goat and bighorn sheep in the high country.

Lacandón Wilderness

Mexico For centuries the Usumacinta River was the only highway into this tropical rain forest in Mexico. Logging and oil exploration have cut roads into the wilderness in recent years, but many square miles of jungle remain. This is true rain forest, saturated with up to 200 inches of rainfall a year. Trees towering 120 feet, and draped with orchids and

bromeliads resound with howler monkeys, toucans, and noisy scarlet macaws. The few native people still living here are descendants of the Maya, whose elaborate civilization collapsed a millennium ago. Maya ruins overgrown with thick vegetation await examination in the forest by archaeologists. Dugout canoes are the only means of transportation in the Usumacinta, with its irregular bottom and frequent rapids. Crocodiles live in the river, and jaguars and ocelots pad the forest floor. The brocket deer is valued for its meat, and the skins of otters, peccaries, and jungle cats are taken by local hunters for sale. Many incursions have been made into the Lacandón, but the 818,384-acre Montes Azules Biosphere Reserve remains relatively pristine.

La Amistad Biosphere Reserve

Costa Rica/Panama This area of both tropical forest and some of the highest nonvolcanic mountains in Central America spills over the borders of Costa Rica and Panama, one of a planned string of "peace parks" intended to save critical wilderness areas. On the Costa Rican side, where protection has been enforced, La Amistad represents the largest protected area in a nation

Badlands

South Dakota The nearly quarter million acres of surrealistic geology were carved by wind and water over millions of years. The area was once an inland sea that laid down layers of marine sediments and silt washed in by numerous rivers that have long since disappeared. After the sea had withdrawn and a vast marshy plain remained, the area was home to a number of prehistoric mammals, including saber-toothed cats, a pig the size of a pony, and a horse with three toes. Their remains have made the Badlands one of the richest Oligocene fossil beds in the world. Eventually, huge volcanoes in the west spread a fine ash over it all. Aridity left a hard, caked surface that eroded into a jagged countryside of castlelike spires, strange shapes, and deep gullies that now make up a much-visited national park. Snakes, bats, and rodents are the most efficient survivors, but in areas where the natural grasslands are recovering from earlier agriculture, bison and pronghorn roam, and bighorn sheep scamper along the high cliffs. The beauty of this unusual landscape can be observed from a car window while driving roads through the area, but many hiking trails also wind through the park.

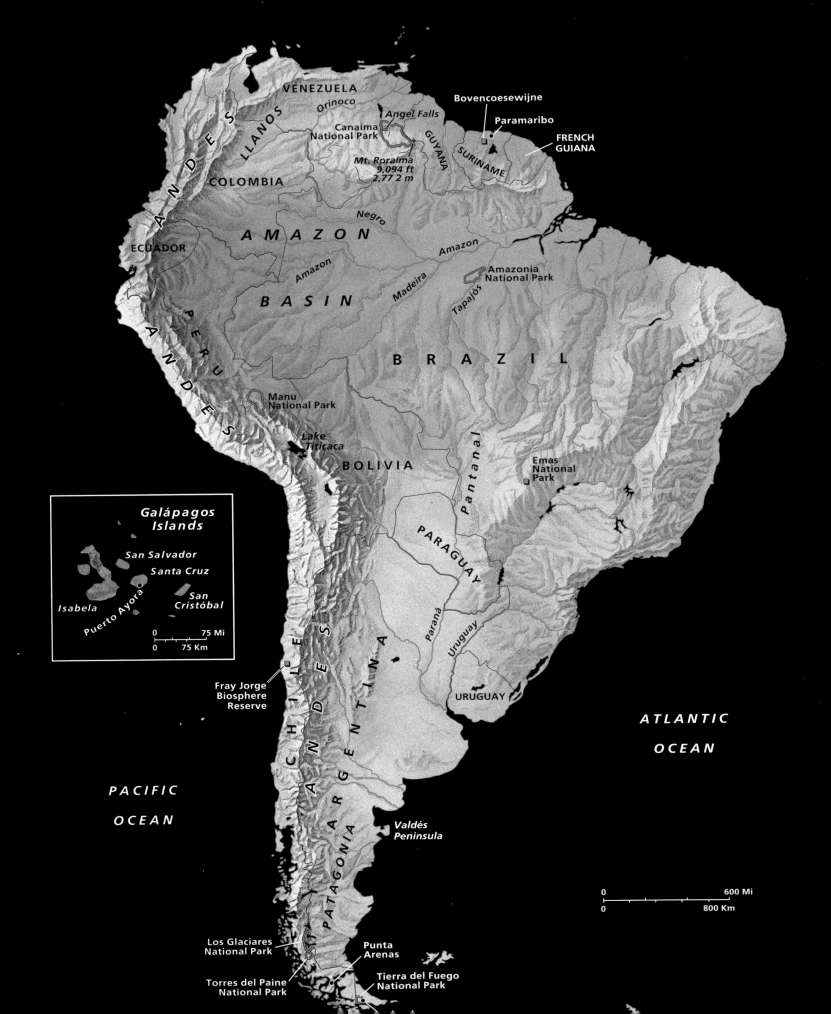

VENEZUELA

Orinoco

Angel Falls

Bovencoesewijne

Paramaribo

Canaima
National Park

GUYANA

SURINAME

FRENCH
GUIANA

LLANOS

Mt. Roraima
9,094 ft
2,77 2 m

COLOMBIA

Negro

A M A Z O N

ANDES

ECUADOR

Amazon

Amazon

Amazonia
National Park

B A S I N

Madeira

Tapajós

PERU

B R A Z I L

ANDES

Manu
National Park

Lake
Titicaca

BOLIVIA

Pantanal

Emas
National
Park

*Galápagos
Islands*

San Salvador

Santa Cruz

PARAGUAY

Isabela

Puerto Ayora

San
Cristóbal

0   75 Mi

0   75 Km

ANDES

Paraná

Uruguay

URUGUAY

ATLANTIC

OCEAN

Fray Jorge
Biosphere
Reserve

CHILE

ARGENTINA

PACIFIC

OCEAN

PATAGONIA

Valdés
Peninsula

Los Glaciares
National Park

Punta
Arenas

Torres del Paine
National Park

Tierra del Fuego
National Park

0   600 Mi

0   800 Km

South America

by David Yeadon

South America is a wild place-lovers' paradise. In a single day of air travel, visitors crossing over the vast 4,500-mile-long Andean Cordillera, the world's longest continuous mountain chain, can observe a spectacular array of distinct ecological environments, from glaciated coastal fjords, steamy mangrove swamps, and dense rain forest to high paramo grasslands, virtually featureless deserts, and towering sea-scoured cliffs. Travelers can also experience a broad range of intriguing wildlife, including the llama-like guanacos and vicunas, giant condors riding the mountain thermals, and large flightless rheas scampering across the plains.

This immense 6.8-million-square-mile landmass contains the richest plant and animal life in the world and encompasses the ultimate wild place, the almost Australia-size Amazon Basin, home to millions of species. Dotted across the 12 nations of South America are more than 700 protected areas, ranging from the vast 11,700-square-mile Canaima National Park in Venezuela to the 50-square-mile Fray Jorge Biosphere Reserve in central Chile.

While only a meager portion of this enormous continent is protected, limited initiatives reflect growing concern on the part of governments for the retention of pristine examples of the continent's rich ecological heritage. As we learn more about the needs of nature from our own research and the timeless insights of indigenous peoples, the necessity of increasing the range and size of protected areas will become dramatically evident and justifiable. Amazonia's current rain forest destruction at the rate of about 5,800 square miles a year is merely one of many threats faced here. Even though an encouraging start has been made, the call to action is both urgent and vital.

Angel Falls, tallest cascade in the world, looks down on clouds as it makes its leap from a tabletop mountain in southern Venezuela. Remote and only partially explored, dozens of these soaring mesas, called tepuis, *harbor plants and animals found nowhere else, some living on a single mountaintop.*

Tepuis

"So tomorrow we disappear into the unknown. This...may be our last word to those who are interested in our fate....I have no doubt...that we are really on the eve of some most remarkable experiences."

Sir Arthur Conan Doyle, *The Lost World*

With these tantalizing words the world-renowned creator of Sherlock Holmes released his new novel, *The Lost World*, in 1912 to an enthusiastic public. It was based upon an intriguing premise. Somewhere on the remote northern fringes of the Amazon Basin, an eccentric professor from England explores a primeval lost world of flat-topped, sheer-sided mountains soaring out of impenetrable jungle. He sees evidence of prehistoric creatures on these misty summits and returns after numerous misadventures to proclaim the existence of a place where time has stood still, enveloping bastions of ancient life-forms long considered extinct but actually protected in perpetuity atop these elusive "islands-in-the-sky."

Sir Arthur's story was partly based on fact. There *is* such a lost world deep in the rain forests south of the Orinoco River in the southeast corner of Venezuela. It is a uniquely strange and mysterious place encompassing more than a hundred mesalike, cloud-bound *tepuis,* many rising suddenly more than 5,000 feet from the forest floor. The highest waterfall on earth, Angel Falls, tumbles 3,212 feet through its own translucent mist from the summit of Auyan-tepui ("devil mountain" in local Indian dialect), the largest of all the mountains with a surface area of some 250 square miles. It is located in Canaima National Park, which covers a small portion of this 500-mile-long, 200,000-square-mile region known locally as La Gran Sabana.

To the south, imposing 9,094-foot Mount Roraima, the tallest tepui in the eastern Venezuela chain, attracts an increasing number of visitors, who scale its rain-doused, moss-coated flanks to a bleak wind- and cloud-whipped summit. Here, exhausted and mud-caked, they enter a badlands labyrinth of lichen-blackened sandstone monoliths carved by the rain. Vegetation is sparse and spiky. Pockets of insect-eating sundew and pitcher plants somehow flourish on platforms of moss and lichen. Black lagoons, bogs, sinkholes, and slimy crags lie in wait for the unwary, and waterfalls tumble hundreds of feet.

Casual tourists are being increasingly discouraged by the Venezuelan park authority from visiting other parts of this still wild and relatively unexplored region. The unique ecosystems of the summits are felt to be far too fragile and valuable to allow unchecked access. While Sir Arthur fantasized about pterodactyls, dinosaurs, and missing-link tribes, reality reveals a more modest but equally entrancing evolutionary process at work here. As many as half of the hundreds of species of orchids, bromeliads, shrubs, and stunted trees, in addition to a wide range of insects, birds, and reptiles, are endemic and have developed in virtually undisturbed isolation over millions of years—in fact, ever since this onetime Gondwanaland plateau of sandstone and quartzite rocks started drifting apart from Africa around 135 million years ago. Indian legends of evil monsters and spirits kept forest tribes well away from the soaring slopes

Gardens of stone on a tepui's summit mimic the monsters and spirits thought to dwell there in Indian beliefs. Carved by rains and rivers, tepuis are sandstone mesas of an eroded plateau (opposite).

Plant life has adapted to the meager nutrients of rocky summits, but fragile specimens are trampled or stolen by growing numbers of human visitors.

and cracked caps of the tepuis.

One outlying tepui, Autana, is considered particularly sacred and boasts a spectacular cave protected by hosts of tarantulas and claimed by the local Indians to be the lair of a particularly ferocious monster. As with many other tepuis, the vertical walls of Autana are thick with a variety of clinging plants that reflect the climate layers and give the monolith a truly

Tepuis

Endemic Species

The isolation of these hundred or so "islands-lost-in-time" has enabled the evolution of scores of endemic species of flora and fauna. Location-specific adaptations over millions of years have also produced forms that exist only on a single tepui, with related but different types found on other summits. It is estimated that as many as half of the species discovered to date do not exist any-where else in the world, and include a thumbnail-size toad that neither hops nor swims, winged but flightless water crickets, and birds such as the greater flower-piercer and the tepui spinetail. Lichen, which blacken the tepuis' pink sandstones, and mosses form vegetation platforms for hundreds of species of orchids, bromeli-ads, and sundews.

primordial character. Indian tales of giant ape men, "tepui-yetis", and more recent stories of Loch Ness-type creatures resembling small plesiosaurs seem totally believable in such surroundings. "How could a place so remote and different *not* have wonderful, fantastic life-forms?" tropical ecologist Dr. Otto Huber said in 1992. "No other region in the world has these kinds of ecosystems at that elevation....On tepuis you have two or three abrupt steps, and each has evolved in its own direction, without all the genetic interchange that normally occurs among neighboring life communities. You find more strange things in very little space."

As with many wild places, the tepuis are facing the familiar challenges of tourist pressures in all guises, including sky divers, para-sailors, balloonists, and one *Guinness Book of World Records* aspirant who bicycled off the edge of Auyan-tepui with a para-chute. Major threats to Canaima National Park include fires caused by natives and tourists, and gold mining that involves the use of high-pressure water hoses. A hydroelectric project for the Caroni River and propos-als to increase tourist facilities in Canaima are creating demands for more conserva-tion measures. Restrictions on airborne and other excur-sions are a promising start. Fortunately, the size and inaccessibility of this region may well ensure that this lost world remains splendidly lost well into the future. "It was a wonderland like nothing on earth," wrote British moun-taineer Hamish MacInnes. And long may it so remain.

Life clings to life atop a tepui, where torrential rains wash away soils. Hardy plants fasten to an island of lichen and moss (below). A dagger-leaved endemic herb (opposite) and an iridescent hummingbird brighten the somber cloud forest.

Rain Forest

By its very nature the tropical rain forest is the richest, most diverse, and most complex biome on the planet and also the least understood by science. Despite decades of careful studies barely one percent of the 155,000 plant species estimated to exist in the world's tropical forests have been thoroughly analyzed. These powerhouses of nature—wet, dense, humid, multilayered, canopied tumults of rapid growth and decomposition—still remain elusive. Their capacities for efficient nutrient recycling, constant regeneration, and the intimate melding of hundreds of plant species—from 200-foot high buttressed giants festooned with epiphytes, orchids, lianas, mosses, and lichens, to low-light understory of ferns, shrubs, saplings, and herbaceous species—make rain forests the most productive vegetation systems on earth. Along with the thousands of species of birds, mammals, reptiles, butterflies and other insects that cohabit in canopies, nature has created an almost miraculous blending of ecosystems linked by complex food chains in which forest organisms are dependent upon one another for mutual survival.

The biological diversity of the rain forest is legendary. One 25-acre area of Malaysian rain forest, for example, can contain more tree species than all of North America. In addition, canopy research suggests that 5 to 30 million insect species may exist there. The biome as a whole may contain over 70 percent of all earth's plant and animal types.

"The great ecosystems are like complex tapestries," said naturalist Gerald Durrell. "A million complicated threads, interwoven, make up the whole picture….What nature cannot cope with is the steady undermining of its fabric by the activities of man." Almost half of the tropical rain forest that once covered about six million square miles of the earth has been destroyed, and the rate of deforestation between 1980 and 1990 was almost double that of the previous decade.

Threats are multitudinous, the most severe being logging, slash-and-burn activities for new farmlands and cattle ranges, mining, pollution, hydroelectric schemes, and flawed "forest management" strategies—all driven by the great unstoppable engines of rapidly increasing human population and spiraling consumer demands. The predicted impact of this destruction is almost too dramatic to contemplate: violent climatic changes through a distortion of rainfall patterns; an alarming increase of carbon dioxide in the atmosphere due to the release of the gas that occurs when deforestation is accomplished by burning, and to the elimination of photosynthesizing, oxygen-

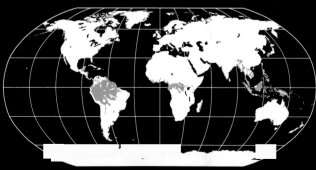

■ **Rain forest**

producing, carbon dioxide-absorbing plants; the destruction of indigenous tribal cultures; and the elimination of vast and still untapped resources for medicine and food.

While the future is uncertain, there are signs of national and international actions to slow the rate of destruction. India, Thailand, and the Philippines have declared their deforestation a national concern, and in Kenya and Colombia tree-planting movements have made headway. But it is clear that we will need an international consensus to save the rain forest.

Green factories of oxygen and moisture, rain forests breathe like lungs for earth. Layers of forest canopy struggle toward sunlight, casting perpetual shade beneath. Native also to Asia and Africa, tropical rain forest finds a large but beleaguered bastion in the Amazon Basin.

Manu

This is the kind of mysterious Eden that many dream of—remote, little explored, full of surprises, teeming with undiscovered forms of wildlife, and home to small groups of nomadic Indians virtually untouched by outside influences. Add to these tantalizing characteristics a dramatic Andes location, dual UNESCO status as a biosphere reserve and world heritage site, a 7,260-square-mile watershed of virgin forest cut by rivers that eventually lead to the great Amazon itself, tales of the Paititi—the "lost city" of the Inca, and you have Peru's remarkable Manu region, one of the world's richest and most biologically diverse environments.

Streams tumble from the 13,000-foot peaks of the Paucartambo Mountains down the eastern slopes through gorges and valleys containing increasingly dense and cloud-bound layers of forest. They ease their flows to join the Manu and the Madre de Dios Rivers, which curl and coil through lowland rain forest to join the Amazon a thousand miles beyond the eastern fringes of this great reserve.

Despite ongoing environmental calamities on our beleaguered planet (even remote Manu was once exploited for latex and is today threatened by encroaching colonization, gold mining, small-scale cattle raising and illegal logging), we occasionally owe ourselves a pat on the back for taking a concerted stand in the name of conservation. While eternal vigilance will always be the key to ongoing success, action to protect most of the Manu watershed within the reserve has enabled the preservation of a large proportion of South America's range of flora and fauna—so many species in fact that the counting is still under way. To date it is estimated that more than 15,000 plant, 200 mammal, 1,000 bird (about 11 percent of the earth's total), and maybe as many as a million different species of insects and other invertebrates flourish within the confines of this amazing region. A forest-canopy insect inventory of two and a half acres of Manu rain forest could easily turn up 40,000 species, including 12,000 different kinds of beetles. More than 70 species of ants have been found on one tree.

Notable here is the mixture of such North American species as deer and bears with ancient South American species such as opossums, armadillos, anteaters, and sloths. The reserve's symbol, the giant harpy eagle, reflects current successes in protecting some of Amazonia's exotic creatures, including

Like breath of the forest, mist hangs over still waters in Peru's Manu National Park. Pristine forest here is protected by the park, which encloses a cross-cut of intact habitats from high Andean slopes to lowland rain forest. Within it lives an astoundingly large portion of the world's plant and animal species.

the condor, hoatzin, blue-headed parrot, giant otter, puma, jaguar, ocelot, spectacled bear, black and spectacled caimans, and the elusive Peruvian huemul deer of the highlands.

The ecological layers of Manu are clear and distinct. On slopes over 11,500 feet is the cold, wind-whipped *puna*—a tundra landscape of tussock grasses, hardy shrubs, and reed-fringed pools beneath the high summits. Furry mammals such as the mountain viscacha and the Andean fox eke out a living from this hard land. Then, slowly merging through misty elfin forests of lichen-clad scrub trees, the puna gives way to the strange diaphanous half-light of the cloud forest filled with lacy bamboo clusters and low twisted-trunk trees smothered in mosses, ferns, and brilliant orchids. These species thrive together in the daytime warmth and rainfall from the almost constant cloud cover. A variety of hummingbirds can be seen, as well as brilliantly colored tanagers, red and black Andean cocks of the rock, and blue-crowned motmots waving their peculiar pendulum-like tail feathers.

Lower down, trees begin to increase in height, and thick underbrush

Manu

Manu

grows in wild profusion beneath a light aerial canopy. Then finally, as the foothills ease out into the broad lowland bowls and plains, comes the tumultuous riot of vegetation and wildlife that characterizes the classic Amazonian tropical rain forest. Here, in this hot, humid zone, dripping in frequent cascades during the rainy season, hundreds of tree species, including tropical cedar, mahogany, and kapok, mix to form the immense 150-foot-high canopy. Emergents, the tallest trees, may rise 200 feet or more, with crowns above the canopy. The dark and breezeless undergrowth below, laced with snakelike lianas and creepers, is home to tapirs, deer, and ground-birds such as curassows and tinamous that feast on fallen fruits and nuts.

But it is the high canopy itself that provides the widest and wildest profusion of plant and animal life. In this storied territory of abundance, hordes of howler monkeys (one of 13 primate species identified in Manu) hurl themselves through the fruit-, flower-, and nut-laden treetops among the toucans and cotingas, the hawks, woodpeckers, and bats, the snakes and lizards, and countless species of insects constantly foraging and feasting— a frenzy of life unmatched in any other non-aquatic environment.

Manu is a truly magnificent slice of ecological purity, offering one of the greatest concentrations of plant and animal diversity on the planet. Despite recent problems with creeping colonization on the south-western edge and an airstrip in the north, it is likely to stay that way.

An avian playground for a thousand species, Manu has no birds more striking than red-and-green macaws (opposite). Among the largest of all parrots, they gather at spots along the river to eat clay, necessary to their diet. Their presence, along with relatives like the white-bellied parrot (below), is testimony to Manu's robust natural health: Many of its species are endangered or extinct elsewhere. The reserve is one of the largest areas of intact and protected rain forest on the planet.

An unlikely candidate for scientific stardom, a land iguana is among the cast of Galápagos characters that helped inspire Charles Darwin's theory of evolution. Jet-era travel has overcome the islands' mid-Pacific isolation, and could overturn their natural balance, already disturbed by alien species.

Galápagos

"Hence, both in space and time, we seem to be brought somewhat near to that great fact—that mystery of mysteries—the first appearance of new beings on this earth." Charles Darwin, in the Galápagos

And this is indeed where it all began—on this 3,000-square-mile Equator-straddling Ecuadorean archipelago containing 13 large wind-torn volcanic islands, 6 smaller islands, and scores of islets, all spewed forth by the joining of three vast tectonic plates 5 million or so years ago and bathed by the nutritious mingling of 3 warm and cold ocean currents. Thanks to a five-week stay here by Charles Darwin in 1835, the Galápagos have become not only the philosophical touchstone of our "origin of species" ideas but also a prime symbol of nature's furious capacity for constant evolution and her vulnerability in the face of man's incessant demands.

Even from his preliminary observations of the amazing variety and evolutionary uniqueness of species and subspecies here from marine iguanas, fur seals, sea lions, and penguins to flightless cormorants, blue-footed boobies, and his famous 13 species of finches—Darwin suspected his theories "would undermine the stability of species" and threaten the comfortable God-centered creationist beliefs that were then the underpinnings of Western man's self-perception. He was right. Even today the doctrinal battles continue—and all because of these tiny creature-filled bits of land, which were "discovered" by the Spanish Bishop of Panama, Tomás de Berlanga, in 1535 and, until very recently, supported a meager human population of less than 2,000.

The intrigued bishop named them Las Islas Encantadas ("the enchanted isles") and so they must have seemed at the time—more than a hundred pristine islands, islets, and rocks where animals originating from South America had evolved unmolested over the years into endemic species reflective of the varied island ecosystems. But then the inevitable intrusions began. From the 17th to the 19th century these islands were primarily the haunt of buccaneers, whalers, and sealers who rejoiced in the profusion of giant tortoises (*galápagos* is the Spanish name for tortoises), which remained alive in ship holds for a year or more without food or water and provided delicious meat for undernourished sailors. Later, settlers brought other forms of environmental plagues—pigs, goats, cats, dogs, and, rats—that destroyed both vegetation and wildlife.

Even today, with the islands' protective labelings as a national park, UNESCO world heritage site and biosphere reserve, and international whale sanctuary, tensions and feuds among politicians, tour operators, smugglers, fishermen, scientists, and conservationists of every hue threaten to disrupt the ecological balance in one of the world's most famous, yet fragile, wild places. A 1994 government ban on the fishing of sluglike sea cucumbers to protect

Galápagos

the species led to protests by machete-wielding fishermen in quaint Puerto Ayora, the islands' largest town. Demands for increased self-government by islanders created more hostilities in 1995 leading to a two-week occupation of the Charles Darwin Research Station and the national park headquarters. In addition tourist visits have soared from 1,000 per year in the early sixties to more than 50,000 in 1994 and, while many come as ecotourists, some are drawn by recreational interests. This, in turn has attracted new immigrants who flock in to capitalize on the unexpected surge of fresh wealth and have

increased the year-round population to 15,000, more than 7 times the 1970 level.

"If there's one place in the world where we should draw a line in the sand, it's the Galápagos," one paleontologist suggested recently. But the line does not yet hold—illegal fishing for sharks, giant tortoises, sea lions, sea urchins, seahorses, and pipefish; the introduction of over 300 non-native plant species; and the ecological threats posed by thousands of free-roaming goats and burros—all contribute to a classic case of eco nomic versus environmental conflict. Most scuba divers—who come to enjoy the abundant marine life of nine-foot manta rays, four-foot moray eels, hammerheads, goatfish, groupers, and 50 endemic species all fed by the plankton-rich currents—would agree with Roger McManus, president of the Washington-based Center for Marine Conservation, that these waters and the islands they surround should be "secure from the short-term follies of humans."

Whether Ecuador, one of South America's poorest nations, can find a satisfactory balance between the demands of islanders and the hopes of the world's scientists and conservationists has yet to be seen.

Airborne or earthbound, the islands' creatures present evolutionary case studies. The slow life of a Galápagos giant tortoise can stretch a hundred years, but some subspecies, isolated on separate islands, face extinction due to introduced predators and grazers. All but a handful of the world's waved albatross nest on the island of Española and engage in an elaborate bonding dance (above). After fledglings depart, they live on the wing over the ocean without touching land for years.

FOLLOWING PAGES: The world's only oceangoing lizards, marine iguanas sun on rocks while lava flows billow into the sea on Fernandina, still growing from volcanism.

Great egrets hunt the waters of the Pantanal in Bolivia and Brazil, largest wetland in the world. With an estimated 650 bird species, the area serves as a major avian nesting ground. Only a small part is protected land; a medley of abuses and a river-dredging plan cloud its future.

Pantanal

Spread across a 55,000-square-mile, border-straddling basin in the heart of the continent is one of South America's strangest regions. A dry and sun-baked savanna from June through October, the Pantanal (Portuguese for "swamp") is flooded by rains and rivers into a vast shallow marshland dotted with forest- and shrub-covered islands for the remainder of the year. There are few regions outside Africa that allow the opportunity to see such a spectacular density of wildlife and vegetation.

This bizarre wetland mosaic of floodplains, permanent rivers, pools, hills, and ridges displays a melding of Amazonian forest and Brazilian savanna, and offers a rich variety of vegetation and life-forms. A Noah's ark mixing of animals can often be seen on the higher islands during the annual water-wilderness season. Pampas deer, marsh deer, greater rheas, boar-like peccaries, families of guinea pig-like capybara (at 130 pounds, the world's largest rodent), tapirs, maned wolves, giant anteaters, armadillos and occasional black howler monkeys forage together among the ant and termite nests, palm groves, and forest thickets above the floodwaters. During the dry season huge flocks of waterbirds—egrets, ibises, wood storks, herons, and jabiru storks (symbol of the Pantanal) jostle for prey concentrated in the contracting ponds.

At first glance, this environment seems safe from violation. Even extensive but low-density cattle ranching has done little to change the essential character of the landscape except for controversial grassland burnings. But, as elsewhere, man-spawned activities are threatening the future of this unique region. The piranha-eating caiman and giant otter populations have been heavily hunted. High market prices for unusual bird species such as the hyacinth macaw have reduced their numbers to fewer than 3,000. Add to these challenges proposals for dam construction, marshland drainage, deforestation, river pollution by erosion, pesticide runoff, toxic waste from gold mining and sugar cane processing and a resultant diminution of the fish population, and one wonders how long this vast natural resource can survive, particularly when less than 2 percent is currently protected by national park status.

While some positive efforts are being made to reverse this degradation, such as commercial caiman farming to reduce rampant poaching, the region's latest threat comes from a proposed 2,130-mile-long river link from Uruguay to western Brazil to "open up South America's heartland to prosperity." Claiming that this region is home to 650 species of birds, 240 varieties of fish, 80 types of mammals, 50 kinds of reptiles, and thousands of plant species, the World Wildlife Fund believes that the project, unless modified, could lead to massive desertification. In response, proponents of the pro-

Pantanal

posal say that the plan would provide landlocked Bolivia and Paraguay with a desperately needed outlet to the Atlantic and dismiss the objections of environmentalists by suggesting that "the benefits far outweigh the ecological costs." A positive dialogue is taking place, and some progress has been made to modify original plans for the project and avoid a major environmental catastrophe. Nevertheless, the waterway project remains a major threat.

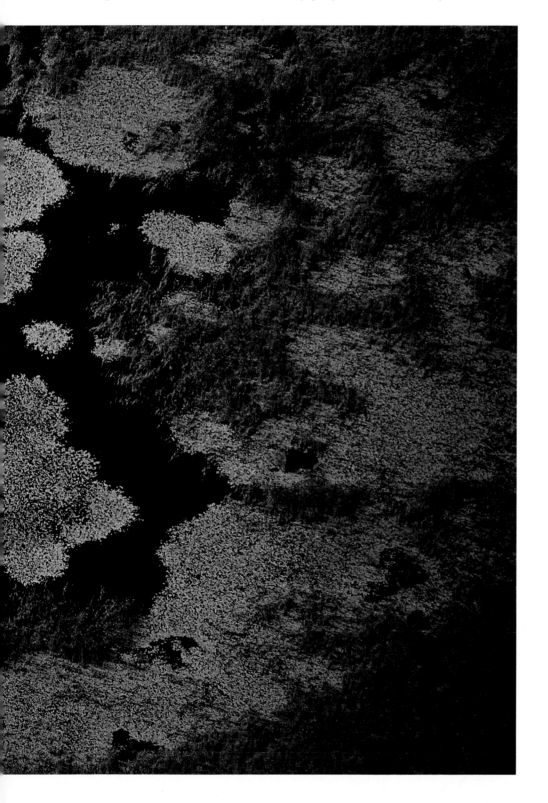

Seasons of wet and dry control the life's pulse of the Pantanal, where a giant water lily unfolds its blossom (above). Lagoons hold water through the dry season (left). When rains come, the inundated area becomes an 55,000-square-mile landlocked sea. Flooding has kept most permanent human habitation at bay, although cattle graze much of the region. Annual dunking and drying makes for rich grasses, undergirding the great biological diversity of the Pantanal.

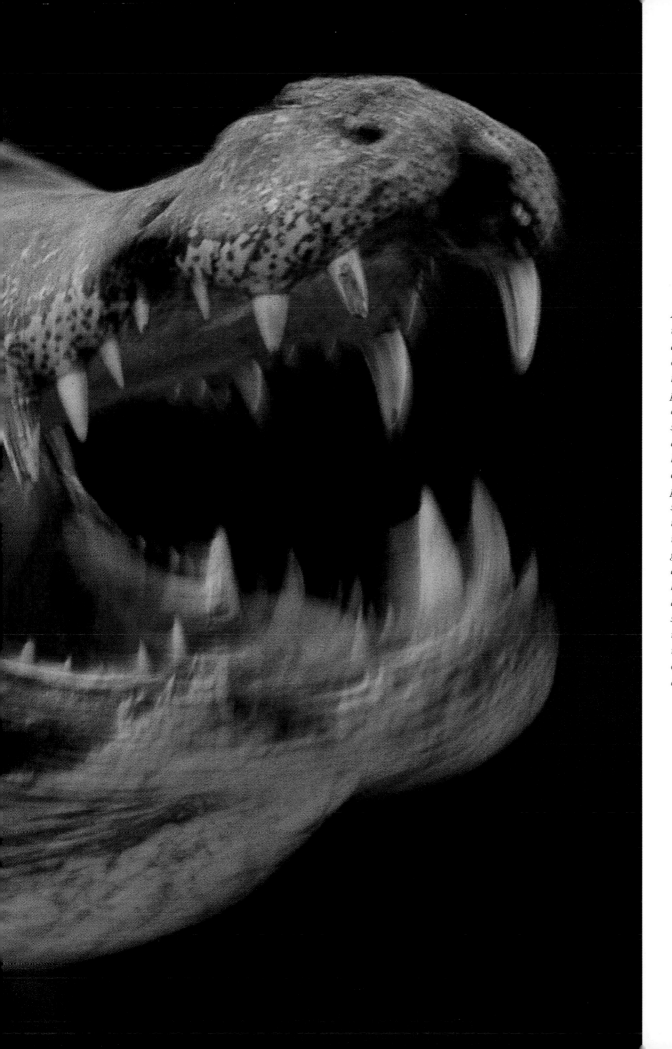

Armed by nature with a fearsome arsenal, a jacare, or caiman, has little defense against poachers who have decimated this subspecies of crocodilian for their hides. Government efforts to control poaching are stymied by the vastness of the region. Jaguars, giant otters, giant anteaters, and hyacinth macaws are among other striking creatures in the Pantanal's multihued palette of colorful characters.

Torres del Paine

It is hard to conceive of other places on earth where a combination of dramatic climatic variations and converging ecosystems have created such a magnificent panoply of landscapes. The bare, torn pinnacles of Chile's Torres del Paine peaks, bathed in brilliant golden sunsets and skimmed by giant condors, are the very stuff of mountaineer fantasies—the Tetons of the Southern Hemisphere. Photographers salivate and fiddle frantically with their f-stops at the prospect of capturing this awesome majesty; tourists flock in the thousands to gaze at the grandeur from the comfort of hotel lounges; backpackers hike through sodden forests to the ice fields of this climactic display of Andean glory. And when you add to all this clear, roaring rivers, secluded lakes, a fjord coastline that even Norwegians envy, and the vast brown-gray infinities of the rain-shadowed Patagonian desert to the east— you begin to understand why this remote, sparsely populated piece of land at the tip of South America is becoming an increasingly sought-after wild-place experience.

The Patagonian desert is the least explored sector of this fascinating region. Named by the Portuguese explorer Ferdinand Magellan in 1520 after the huge hide moccasins worn by the Tehuelche Indians, Patagonia stems from *patagones*—the Spanish word for "big feet." Beyond the beech forests and lakes at the foot of the Andes, haunts of deer and waterfowl, this vast 260,000-square-mile desert eases into bunchgrass steppes and endless arid plains scoured by fierce "broom of God" winds and choking dust storms. The British explorer-mountaineer Eric Shipton accurately declared it to be a "land of tempest." In the northern sector man-high thorny thickets are widely spaced across bare soil, but as one moves south to the drier zones, scattered knee-high bushes eventually give way to the eye-scouring emptiness of endless gravel desert.

In such an inhospitable land, cut by broad deep valleys carved by furious melts between ice ages, it is surprising to find evidence of wildlife particularly when places of refuge and shade seem so sparse. But nature as usual has stimulated innovative adaptions: The guanaco, a humpless llama-like cousin of the camel, and Darwin's rhea, a three-foot-tall, ostrich-like flightless bird, have remarkable capacities for speedy escapes from predators, as does the mara, a rodent which has developed the body shape and

Newly sprung from snow and glacial melt, a stream starts on its way to the sea in Chile's Torres Del Paine National Park in Patagonia. Near the southern tip of the Andes, with Antarctica not far away, the chilly, windswept region presents a wild and austere beauty.

long legs of a hare and digs burrows for safety. Other animals possessing unusually strong limbs and claws for burrowing include the pichi armadillo and various species of gopher-like tuco-tuco that spend much of their time underground to avoid the scourge of peregrine falcons and eagles. In response, predators such as the skinny Patagonian weasel have become adept burrow hunters, while gray foxes and 150-pound pumas utilize stealth and speed to hunt their prey—which in turn requires the nimble guanaco to run as fast as a race horse.

Running can be a little too arduous in the Torres del Paine National Park itself, especially for humans who come to hike the spectacular but challenging mountain scenery. Located around 220 miles north of Punta Arenas, the region's most world-renowned features are the soaring granite

Torres del Paine

and shale batholith mountain towers of Paine Grande (10,007 feet) and the twin horns of Cuernos del Paine, which rise abruptly above the broad plains where horsemen tend flocks of widely scattered sheep.

From the glacier-carved peaks, runoff streams tumble through rain-soaked forests on the highland plateaus to lower meadows of ox-eye daisies and foxgloves, and finally to the arid plains. In the dramatic forested fjords of the west the dainty 15-inch-high pudu deer was saved from extinction by the creation of 700-square-mile Torres del Paine National Park in 1962. The area became a biosphere reserve in 1978. As a result of these and other conservation efforts more than 40 species of mammals and 435 different varieties of birds, including black-necked swans, buff-necked ibises, flamingoes, condors, and falcons, can be seen within the park. One writer, amazed by the rich variety of scenery and wildlife here, claimed that "Torres del Paine is the sort of park that changes its visitors by setting standards of sheer sensory impact against which all other parks are thereafter measured." The park authority's exemplary sensitivity to the oft-competing needs of visitors and the environment suggests that such an accolade is well-deserved.

A relative of camels, a guanaco (opposite) might fall prey to a puma, but finds sanctuary in the park from human hunting that devastated the population. Swift and surefooted, guanacos can weigh 250 pounds and stand as South America's tallest mammals. Along with guanacos, Darwin's rheas (above) rank among the park's wildlife stars. The flightless birds have also rebounded in the park from numbers made dangerously small by hunting and egg-gathering.

FOLLOWING PAGES: The granite fastness of Cuernos del Paine's twin horns gleams in morning light like castles guarding the end of South America.

Other Wild Places

Bovencoesewiine

Suriname Nestled on the Atlantic coast between Guyana and French Guiana, Suriname is a former Dutch colony with a polyglot population of less than half a million, and the gateway to a neotropical rain forest of more than two million square miles. One recent visitor, amazed by the biogeographical riches here, claimed that "Suriname is to flora and fauna what Fort Knox is to gold. Mother Nature has deposited a stockpile of her finest treasures here." More than 95 percent of the country is rain forest, with 14 parks and reserves providing havens for 244 species of butterflies, 674 types of birds, 8 types of monkeys, and an encyclopedic array of trees and other plants.

Conservationists are trying to establish an ecotourism industry as an alternative to logging the rain forest. There are several reserves that are still wild and almost unknown, including Bovencoesewijne, 100 square miles of sand savanna and inland swamp along

ALLIGATOR ON LILY PAD IN AMAZON, BRAZIL

the beautiful black-water Coesewijne River. Here, caimans and manatees can be found, along with giant river otters. Orchids fill the riverbank woodlands along with abundant bird species. Although only 90 minutes by car from the capital, Paramaribo, facilities are primitive, but visitors who come prepared can enjoy a unique "eco-experience."

Emas National Park

Brazil In the enormous forested wilderness of Brazil, the 500-square-mile Emas National Park appears as a tiny dot on the map between the Amazon and Paraná River basins. Access is difficult, particularly during the December to March rainy season. Biting insects and venomous snakes abound, and brush fires are notorious for their destructiveness. And yet, those seriously in search of one of South America's most varied and richly populated wildlife zones will be amply rewarded with open grasslands, wooded plains, and narrow gallery forests filled with rheas, pampas deer, peccaries, and monkeys. Also found here are endangered wolves, jacamari, toucans, macaws, parrots, and at least 170 other bird species. Nearly 800 species of trees and shrubs have been identified at Emas, but the most memorable features are the hundreds of thousands of brick-red termite mounds, some reaching ten feet in height and more or less evenly distributed across the vast plains, creating an earthly paradise for the seven-foot-long giant anteater and his cousin, the lesser anteater. Nineteenth-century European explorers came here hoping to find a pecuniary paradise in the form of diamonds. They failed, and the region was eventually safeguarded against mining and farming and protected as a unique Eden-like haven. Brazil's Emas National Park is a challenging place to explore—but well worth the effort.

Amazonia National Park

Brazil While Brazil has an active national park program that reflects an interest in preserving its immense ecological heritage, little more than three percent of the nearly United States-size nation is currently protected as parks, reserves, and other zones. The country's liberal rain forest development policies have alarmed conservationists worldwide and while this park was established in 1974 to preserve a rich sampling of the earth's greatest natural resources, its area of under 3,800 square miles represent less than 0.2 percent of the enormous Amazon basin.

Nonetheless it is a splendid (if difficult) place to visit, showcasing the biodiversity of basin ecosystems. In the northern part of the park, light-seeking epiphytes drape the upper branches of the dense-canopied dryland forest, where giant trees can reach 260 feet. With all but one percent of sunlight blocked in some places, thin ground cover struggles in perpetual shade. Undergrowth is thick in *igapó*, or marsh forest; trees and bushes here have buttress or prop roots. The *cipós* forest, tangled with vines and ferns, is a "movie jungle," dark and steamy. Hung with lianas, bromeliads, and orchids, gallery forests along the riverbanks are flooded periodically. The clear Rio Tapajos, one of the basin's most beautiful rivers, skirts this rich and primitive wilderness where over a million species of animal, insect, and plant life flourish.

Los Glaciares National Park

Argentina Admittedly it's a long journey to the storm-battered wilds of Andean Patagonia but, to gauge by the thousands of hikers, climbers, and sightseers who venture here annually, this 2,300-square-mile national park rewards such efforts generously. The classic vista is looking westward at sunrise from the shores of the 50-mile-long Lago Viedma. Bathed in fresh pink and golden rays, the imposing ice-gouged peak of Mount Fitz Roy soars two miles into the crystal morning air, asserting itself as one of

MAGELLAN PENGUINS, PUNTA TOMBO, ARGENTINA

the most striking of Andean mountains. Notorious as a challenge for climbers, the peak was finally conquered in 1952, and others in this dramatic cluster of needle peaks, including the ice-capped Cerro Torre, have reluctantly allowed a handful of ascents.

While the northern peaks attract the adventurers, the 540-square-mile Lago Argentino in the southern portion of the park is ideal for more relaxing launch trips to the enormous glacier fingers that calve their icebergs into its turquoise waters. The 30-mile-long Upsala Glacier is the largest, but Glacier Moreno, one of the world's few advancing glaciers, can be reached on foot as it creaks and groans on its way to the lake. Those seeking true solitude normally camp around Lago Roca in the far south, renowned for its soaring condors, sheldgeese, buff-necked ibis, austral parakeets, and torrent ducks. Tradition has it that those who eat the berries of the calafate shrub will inevitably return to this region.

Tierra del Fuego National Park

Argentina It's hard to imagine any place else on earth where a soul-smashing combination of hurricane-winds, sudden downpours, dense fogs, and mazelike and unpopulated landscapes laced with sphagnum bogs has created a region less hospitable for the average traveler. And yet the more adventurous come in increasing numbers every year to the Alpine-flavored town of Ushuaia, drawn by Tierra del Fuego's fjords, glaciers, and snow-capped peaks. The national park here is renowned for its southern beech forest, a temperate rain forest, and its profusion of birdlife, including condors, albatross, great grebes, black-necked swans, steamer ducks, and rare species such as ashy-headed geese and the endemic ruddy-headed geese. Appalled by the greedy grass-eating appetites of such birds, frantic sheepmen had them declared "a national plague" in 1972 and almost eradicated some species. In similar fashion the island beech forests have suffered from rampant logging, and contact with early settlers destroyed almost all of the four Indian tribes whose abundant fires had led Ferdinand Magellan to name the region "Land of Fire" in 1520.

Charles Darwin, whose *Beagle* passed through the narrow southern channel of Tierra del Fuego (now named the Beagle Channel) in 1832 recorded in his journal that "a single glance at the landscape was sufficient to show me how widely different it was from any thing I had ever beheld." Similar sentiments linger in the souls of today's travelers who explore the wild tip of South America.

Valdés Peninsula

Argentina Although to many intrepid travelers Argentina's Patagonia is a wealth of stunning wildernesses, the author W. H. Hudson described its vast scrubland plains as "universal, unrelieved grayness" and a disgruntled novelist and travel writer, Paul Theroux, declared them to be "nothingness itself." The wind-flayed Valdés Peninsula, a Rhode Island-size extrusion attached by a narrow thread of land to the east coast, reinforces all these points of view. This scrubby territory of bare hills and mesa-like plains, salt flats, and towering coastal cliffs appears to be the very epitome of bleakness. The triangular washboard road around the peninsula, however, with key viewing places at Puerto Pirámides, Punta Delgada, Caleta Valdés, and Punta Norte, reveals amazing seashore and seaborne cornucopias of wildlife. Endangered southern right and killer whales, dolphins, sea lions, fur seals, penguins, and enormous 8,000-10,000 pound elephant seals can all be found in the waters off the peninsula. Such land-based creatures as guanacos, rheas, roadrunner-like tinamous, and maras (Patagonian hares) are a little more elusive than their coastal companions, the Magellanic "jackass" penguins (they bray like donkeys). These are found by the thousand at Punta Tombo and Cabo Dos Bahías to the south of the peninsula and seem to welcome humans, only pecking when intruders become too familiar.

This remarkable region is one of South America's most unusual wildlife showcases—a rich nirvana in an austere wilderness.

About the Authors

Noel Grove, a member of the Society's staff for 25 years, is a freelance writer who has authored 28 articles for the NATIONAL GEOGRAPHIC and contributed chapters to four other National Geographic Society books. He is the author of *Wild Lands for Wildlife: America's National Refuges.*

Elisabeth B. Booz, born in London, spent many years in Asia and now lives in France and the United States. A member of the Society of Woman Geographers, she has written several books, including comprehensive travel guides to New Zealand and Tibet.

Patrick R. Booz is a freelance writer who lives in Sweden. He holds a degree in Asian Studies from the University of Wisconsin and reports frequently on Asia, but his interest in history and geography has taken him several times to Africa.

David Yeadon is the author/illustrator of over 20 travel books, the most recent being *Lost Worlds: Exploring the Earth's Remote Places* and *The Back of Beyond: Travels to the Wild Places of the Earth.* He is a freelance travel feature writer for NATIONAL GEOGRAPHIC TRAVELER, the *Washington Post,* and other publications.

Michael Parfit is the author of four books, including one about Antarctica—*South Light: A Journey to the Last Continent.* He has traveled to Antarctica seven times, and has piloted light aircraft as far north as Ellesmere Island.

Suzanne Chisolm is a writer and consulting economist. A Canadian, she has worked in Estonia, Latvia, Lithuania, London, and Prague. She is presently at work on a study of Inuit land claims and settlements in the Canadian Artic.

Acknowledgments

The Book Division wishes to thank the many individuals, groups, and organizations mentioned or quoted in this book for their help and guidance.

In addition we are grateful to Cosimo Barletta; Mick Blackman; Tim Cansfield-Smith; E. Tazewell Ellett, Jr.; Mike Garner; Gonzalo Castro, Lu Ann Dietz, and Carlos Vallecillo, World Wildlife Fund; Chris Done; Terry Erwin, Smithsonian Institution; Alejandro Grajal, Wildlife Conservation Society; Keith Hockey; the staff of the International Center for Antarctic Information and Research; Suzanne Iudicello, Center for Marine Conservation; Andrzej Kassenberg, Institute for Sustainable Development; Lucia Levendis; Beth Marks, The Antarctica Project; Greg Miles; Charles Munn; Mariana Valqui Munn; Czeslaw Okolow; Ewan Patterson; Lisa Pickel, Embassy of Australia; John Pritchard; Luciano Rota; Margie Scanlon; Amy Shearer; Craig Sholley; Jonathan Stacey, Scottish Natural Heritage; Peter Stanton; Carlos Urdiales; John Watkins; Kim Wong.

Photo Credits

Cover, Art Wolfe; 1-3 (both) Frans Lanting/Minden Pictures; 4-5 David Muench; 6-7 Frans Lanting/Minden Pictures; 10-11 Jean-Paul Ferrero/Ardea London; 12-13 Tom Walker/Tony Stone Images; 14-15 Art Wolfe; 16-17 Frans Lanting/Minden Pictures; 18-19 Christopher Arnesen/Tony Stone Images; 22-27 (all) Frans Lanting/Minden Pictures; 28-29 Frans Lanting/Minden Pictures; 29 Art Wolfe; 30-37 (all) Michael Nichols; 38-45 (all) Jim Brandenburg/Minden Pictures; 46-47 Michael Nichols; 48 Michael Nichols; 48-49 Richard Packwood/Oxford Scientific Films; 49-51 (all) Michael Nichols; 52-53 Art Wolfe; 55 Renee Lynn/Tony Stone Images; 56-57 Art Wolfe; 58 Robert Caputo; 59 (upper) Tom Brakefield/DRK Photo; 59 (lower) Robert Caputo; 60 Frans Lanting/Minden Pictures; 60-61 Robert Caputo/Aurora; 62 (both) Frans Lanting/Minden Pictures; 63 (left) Art Wolfe; 63 (right) George Steinmetz; 66-67 Niall Benvie/Oxford Scientific Films; 68 (upper) Mark Hamblin/Oxford Scientific Films; 68 (lower) R. Sorensen & J. Olsen/NHPA; 69 Niall Benvie/Oxford Scientific Films; 70-72 (both) Jeffrey Aaronson/Network Aspen; 73 (upper) Jeffrey Aaronson/Network Aspen; 73 (lower) J. & J. Blassi/INCAFO; 74-75 Vincente Garcia Canseco/NHPA; 76 Jean-Paul Ferrero/Ardea London; 78-79 (both) B. & C. Alexander; 80-87 (all) Raymond Gehman; 88-89 (all) Toni Anzenberger/Agency Anzenberger Vienna; 92-96 (all) Frans Lanting/Minden Pictures; 97 (upper) Frans Lanting; 97 (lower) Frans Lanting/Minden Pictures; 98-99 James L. Stanfield; 100-101 Thomas J. Abercrombie; 101 James L. Stanfield; 102-105 (both) Art Wolfe/Tony Stone Images; 106 William Thompson; 107 Chris Noble; 108-109 Art Wolfe; 109 Robb Kendrick; 110-111 Richard Kirby/Oxford Scientific Films; 112-113 Sarah Leen; 114 Art Wolfe/Tony Stone Images; 114-115 Art Wolfe; 116-117 (both) Sarah Leen; 118-119 Melvyn Goldstein and Cynthia Beall; 120-123 (all) George B. Schaller; 124-125 (both) George Steinmetz; 128-129 Sam Abell, National Geographic Photographer; 130-131 Paul Chesley; 131 Paul Chesley/Photographers Aspen; 132 Paul Chesley/Photographers Aspen; 132-133 Belinda Wright/DRK Photo; 134-135 David Doubilet; 136-137 Jean-Paul Ferrero/Ardea London; 138-141 (all) David Doubilet; 142-143 Sam Abell, National Geographic Photographer; 144 Michael Fogden/DRK Photo; 145 (upper) Stephen J. Krasemann/DRK Photo; 145 (center & lower) Michael & Patricia Fogden; 146-147 Sam Abell, National Geographic Photographer; 149 Christopher Arnesen/Tony Stone Images; 150-151 José Azel/Aurora; 151 Gary R. Jones/Bruce Coleman, Inc.; 152-153 David Robert Austen; 154 David Hiser/Photographers Aspen; 155 (upper) Christopher Arnesen/Tony Stone Images; 155 (lower) Art Wolfe/Tony Stone Images; 158-159 Frans Lanting/Minden Pictures; 160 Kim Heacox; 161 (upper) José Azel/Aurora; 161 (lower) Kim Heacox/DRK Photo; 162-163 Wolfgang Kaehler; 164 (left & right) Frans Lanting/Minden Pictures; 164 (lower) Tui De Roy/Bruce Coleman, Inc.; 164-165 Kim Heacox; 165 (left & center) Wolfgang Kaehler; 165 (right) Frans Lanting/Minden Pictures; 166-167 Vladimir Vyatkin; 168 (upper) Vladimir Vyatkin; 168 (lower) B. & C. Alexander; 169 Vladimir Vyatkin; 170-171 D. Parer & E. Parer-Cook/Ardea London; 172-177 (all) Jim Brandenburg/Minden Pictures; 178-179 Tom Bean; 180-181 Art Wolfe; 181 Michio Hoshino/Minden Pictures; 182-183 Art Wolfe/Tony Stone Images; 183 Michio Hoshino/Minden Pictures; 184 Frans Lanting/Minden Pictures; 184-185 Malcolm Hanes/Bruce Coleman, Inc.; 188-189 Art Wolfe; 190-191 (all) Stephen J. Krasemann/DRK Photo; 192-193 David Muench; 193 Jay Dickman; 194-195 José Azel/Aurora; 196 Tom Till/DRK Photo; 197 Larry Ulrich; 198 Randy Olson; 198-199 Wolfgang Kaehler; 200 Darrell Gulin/DRK Photo; 200-201 Art Wolfe; 201 D. Robert Franz/Planet Earth Pictures; 202-203 Carr Clifton/Minden Pictures; 204-205 David Muench/Tony Stone Images; 206-207 Carr Clifton/Minden Pictures; 208-209 Harald Sund; 210 Jim Zipp/Ardea London; 211 Art Wolfe; 212 Ric Ergenbright; 213 Harald Sund; 214-215 James Randklev/Tony Stone Images; 216-217 Annie Griffiths Belt; 218-219 Melissa Farlow; 220-221 Wendell Metzen/Bruce Coleman, Inc.; 221 Melissa Farlow; 222-223 Wendell Metzen/Bruce Coleman, Inc.; 224-226 (both) Art Wolfe; 227 (upper) Jeff Foott/DRK Photo; 227 (lower) Annie Griffiths Belt; 228-229 David Muench; 231 Charles Krebs/Tony Stone Images; 234-237 (all) Jay Dickman; 238 Jay Dickman; 238-239 Uwe George; 239 Jay Dickman; 240-241 Loren McIntyre; 242 Frans Lanting/Minden Pictures; 244 (both) Michael & Patricia Fogden; 245-247 (all) Frans Lanting/Minden Pictures; 248-249 Michio Hoshino/Minden Pictures; 250-251 Tui De Roy/Bruce Coleman, Inc.; 251 Dieter & Mary Plage; 252-253 Tui De Roy; 254-259 (all) Frans Lanting/Minden Pictures; 261 Hans Strand/Tony Stone Images; 262 Günter Ziesler; 263 Wolfgang Kaehler; 264-265 Hans Strand/Tony Stone Images; 266 Will & Deni McIntyre/Tony Stone Images; 267 Günter Ziesler.

Index

Boldface indicates illustrations

National Geographic's last wild places / prepared by the Book Division, National Geographic Society.

    p.   cm.

   Includes index.

    ISBN 0-7922-3500-2 (reg.). --   ISBN 0-7922-3502-9 (deluxe)

    1. Natural history. 2. Natural history--Pictorial works.

  I. National Geographic Society (U.S.). Book Division.

QH45.5.N35 1996

508--dc20

96-22973

Composition for this book by the National Geographic Society Book Division with the assistance of the Typographic section of National Geographic Production Services, Pre-Press Division. Printed by Webcrafters, Inc., Madison, Wisconsin. Bound by Inland Press, Menomee Falls, Wisconsin. Color separations by Graphic Arts Service, Inc, Nashville, Tennessee; Lanman Progressive Co., Washington, D.C.; North American Color, Portage, Michigan.